Mindfulness for Beginners

Mindfulness for Beginners

4 Weeks to Everyday Peace, Gratitude, and Focus

Ashley Sharp

ROCKRIDGE
PRESS

For general information on our other products and services or to obtain technical support, please contact
our Customer Care Department within the United States at (866) 744-2665, or outside the United States at
(510) 253-0500.

Rockridge Press publishes its books in a variety of electronic and print formats. Some content that appears in
print may not be available in electronic books, and vice versa.

TRADEMARKS: Rockridge Press and the Rockridge Press logo are trademarks or registered trademarks of Callisto
Media Inc. and/or its affiliates, in the United States and other countries, and may not be used without written
permission. All other trademarks are the property of their respective owners. Rockridge Press is not associated
with any product or vendor mentioned in this book.

Interior and Cover Designer: Erin Yeung
Art Producer: Tom Hood
Editor: Erin Nelson
Production Editor: Rachel Taenzler

Ilustrations © Tom Bingham 2020, pp. 24, 40, 43, 79, 81, 103, 114, 123, 145; all other illustrations @ Wilda Mae
Studio 2020.

ISBN: Print 978-1-64739-519-3 | eBook 978-1-64739-520-9

Ro

For Joe, my partner in love and life.

Contents

Because joy and life exist nowhere but the present.

— *MAXINE HONG KINGSTON*

Introduction

Right now, you have everything you need to get started on your mindfulness journey. With mindfulness, we start as we are, where we are in this very moment.

Maybe you are looking for inner peace, to improve your relationships, or to enhance gratitude for the world around you. Maybe you are curious about mindfulness after hearing about it from a family member, co-worker, or friend. You might be new to the idea of mindfulness, or you might want to energize your practice. In any case, this book serves as a door into a richer, more present life.

What you'll find here are tools to cultivate awareness. For every human, life is both challenging and rewarding, painful and delightful. In these pages, we'll create room for the entire spectrum. So, what does this mean on a practical level?

The practice of mindfulness gives us a way to make sense of life. It allows us to act with more skill and ease, whether we are changing a diaper, dealing with difficult co-workers, or protesting injustice. Mindfulness is the ground from which intentional, wise actions spring. It creates the conditions for growth and for doing what needs to be done in your life.

Mindfulness practice is just that: practice. I always remind people that mindfulness is considered to be a "practice" not a "perfect." This means that mindfulness is a process that doesn't have a determined final outcome. It is an ongoing process with room for experimentation, goof-ups, and continuing effort.

My mindfulness story began about 25 years ago when I started practicing yoga. I loved the physical aspects of yoga, yet found the tranquility that I felt during my practice disappeared once I stepped off of the mat. I wanted to know how to bring the teachings of equanimity and compassion, which I had experienced in my body through the yoga practice, into my daily life—I needed support in my everyday relationships, emotions, and work.

Around that same time, I discovered mindfulness meditation when attending Monday night classes with Jack Kornfield at Spirit Rock Meditation Center. I found that the practice of mindfulness complemented my physical yoga practice. Yoga asana helped me understand the experience of benevolence and connectedness, whereas mindfulness meditation helped me understand what was getting in the way of that in my daily life.

As I began to practice mindfulness, my perspective shifted and my relationship to experience changed. I was more often able to remember that everything is always changing—whether my mood, the small irritations, or even the difficult circumstances. When I remember that everything is in a state of flux, I can savor the delightful, love the people around me, and let go of the difficulties. With mindfulness, I remember to practice compassion for the foibles in myself and others. I have learned (most of the time!) how to pause before reacting to small or large events. A pause gives space for a response instead of a knee-jerk reaction, which most often exacerbates the situation. Over time, I have become more and more interested in what I can offer to the world. And most importantly, I have begun to understand that I belong to the world and the world belongs to me.

Once I saw the power of mindfulness in my own life, I started attending many days and then months of silent meditation retreats in order to solidify my practice and deepen the habit of mindfulness. I began my training as a mindfulness teacher in an 18-month program designed for yoga teachers. Next, I attended a two-year program through Spirit Rock Meditation Center called the Dedicated Practitioners Program to study the roots and context of mindfulness. Later, I was nominated for and then attended a two-year teaching program through Spirit Rock Meditation Center called Community Dharma Leaders. Over the years, I have taught mindfulness in both big and small groups in corporate and private settings. I particularly enjoy introducing the practices of mindfulness to beginners because of the immediate benefit and support people see in their lives.

Like all things, we increase mindfulness when we create supportive conditions rather than trying to force things with willpower during times of stress. In fact, willpower alone cannot get us very far, especially when we are running on empty. Our minds are powered by *habits*. It takes 21 days to start a new habit. Investing time with the practices in this book will set you up for a solid understanding of the practice and power of mindfulness. It's my hope you'll come to see how, in the next four weeks, mindfulness practice can serve you in tangible and spiritual ways in the everyday.

As you begin (or continue) a mindfulness practice, you bring your whole world with you. Your joys and disappointments, your triumphs and heartbreaks, have all led you to this moment. Welcome.

How to Use This Book

Many years ago, a student told me that she found mindfulness to be helpful with potty training her child and with her relationship with her mother-in-law. I have heard over and over how transformative mindfulness can be, whatever the situations we find ourselves in throughout our lives. However, the habits and skills of mindfulness take time and intention to learn.

Some students prefer to do a formal mindfulness meditation practice and forget to integrate mindfulness into daily life. Other students find themselves skipping the more formal or time-based daily mindfulness meditation and only practice mindfulness in real-world situations. While both of these methods do work, I have noticed that students who incorporate both a formal mindfulness meditation and daily-life practices into their process receive the most benefit in the shortest amount of time. I have created a plan for you that incorporates mindfulness meditation and daily-life exercises.

Introductory material dives into mindfulness and what exactly it is: how to meditate, how to sit, how to breathe, and how to think about meditation. As you embark upon this journey of mindfulness, it can be very helpful to set aside a bit of time every single day to do a formal meditation practice in order to sharpen your awareness and create the best possible results. This steadfast commitment to developing these skills will help your practice blossom, if you are just starting out, and flourish, if continuing on the path.

From here, we launch into the four-week meditation plan for beginners, broken down by week in order to jump-start your habit in an easy, manageable way. There are 28 days, or 4 weeks, of daily instructions, inspiration, and guidance. You can hop around to the exercise that best suits you in the moment, or you can start at the beginning and work your way through to the end. Remember that practicing when the stakes are low can be very helpful in the development of mindfulness so that the skills will be available to you when things heat up. This is the key to maintaining balance.

The exercises and meditations are designed to support mindfulness in every aspect of your life. During Week 1, you'll start at the beginning, taking a closer at mindfulness and the body. Week 2 brings the practice into your home. Because all of us spend our days engaged in some type of work, Week 3 enters into exercises and meditations designed to support you in your working life, whatever "work" means to you. Finally, in the last week, mindfulness practices will take you out into the world—whether that is in traffic, at the park, or at the grocery store.

Mindfulness is a tool that can be used in conjunction with other therapies and medications as needed for physical or mental illness. However, mindfulness is not a substitute for medical care. Please note that the present moment is sometimes intense; we all need help managing it at times. Remove shame around help if you need it. Meditation is counteracted if you are experiencing psychosis and is never a substitute for prescribed medication or qualified medical care.

Understanding Mindfulness

Renowned scholar and clinician Jon Kabat-Zinn defines mindfulness as the state of mind and heart that arises from the technique of paying attention in a particular way, "on purpose, in the present moment, nonjudgmentally."

This sounds so simple, right? It is. And, at the same time, it is hard to remember to do. This brings us to the first facet of mindfulness, which is remembering. That's it. Remembering to do it. Once you can remember to pay attention to what is happening, you are already leading a more mindful life.

Mindfulness involves directly experiencing and paying attention to both our inside and outside worlds rather than reacting to ideas, views, or judgments about what is happening. We can be mindful of internal experiences such as body sensations, emotions, moods, and thoughts. We can also pay attention to external factors such as sounds, sights, and what is happening in our immediate environment. You can even practice paying attention right now while reading this. You can be aware that you are reading, how your hands feel, and the touch of your back end wherever you are seated. This paying attention to what is happening right now—reading this book wherever you might be, however you might be feeling—this is not your *idea* about what should or should not be happening right now; this is mindfulness of the present moment.

Mindfulness is inclusive, respectful, and is a practice of non-judgment. For these reasons, many teachers refer to it as "kind attention."

The answer to having a better life is not about getting a better life, it's just about changing how we see the one we have right now.

— ANGEL KYODO WILLIAMS

How Mindfulness Works

Mindfulness allows an intimate connectivity with life. It leads to more humor and ease, to more capacity to meet life just as it is, and allows for more space to witness what is happening without any pressure to react.

This happens because mindfulness opens a window into the details of how the mind is working and reacting to life. When we begin to see more clearly what is actually happening inside and around us, insight and resiliency naturally arise. Seeing clearly removes the cobwebs of misunderstanding and delusion.

What we experience when we sit down to meditate or when we take a moment to be mindful might not be all that different from the moments before. But the viewpoint and relationship to our experience is. Mindfulness shifts our perspective.

The expansiveness and harmony people tend to feel when they engage with mindfulness practice is possible because we have the innate capacity to grow and learn. Scientists call this rewiring of the brain "neuroplasticity." We are never too old for this. It is never too late, nor too early, to start on the path of mindfulness.

Its teachings are available to anyone, at any time in one's life.

For the past several decades, researchers have studied the brains of people like you who train in mindfulness. They've found measurable changes in the brain and body that account for:

- Improved memory

- Improved focus

- Reduction in stress

- Improved creativity

- Improved mental health

- Improved compassion and compassionate activity

The benefits of mindfulness have long been available to humans. Yet you must try the practices yourself to reap the rewards.

A Mindfulness Journey around the World

The roots of mindfulness are deeply entwined with Hindu and Buddhist practices. Mindfulness began as a practice that was part of an entire way of life, including training in ethics and the cultivation of both generosity and simplicity. Over the centuries, mindfulness and meditation practices have spread across the world. Because of its ability to apply to so many people and situations, today mindfulness is often taught and practiced separate from any religious tradition.

Many people credit the popularization of mindfulness in the United States to the work of Jon Kabat-Zinn, a doctor who, in 1979, developed Mindfulness Based Stress Reduction (MBSR) to release anxiety, depression, and stress-related health issues. In the 1980s, mindfulness principles began to move into therapeutic circles with modalities such as Dialectical Behavior Therapy (DBT). The spiritual leader of Tibet, the Dalai Lama, has taken a keen interest in the intersection of science and Buddhist teachings, instigating and supporting years of research into meditation and mindfulness.

What Is Mindfulness Based Stress Reduction (MBSR)?

MBSR is an eight-week program developed by Jon Kabat-Zinn that trains people in mindfulness. Participants are asked to practice mindfulness at home (45 minutes daily for at least six days per week) and attend a one-day retreat to help deepen their understanding and solidify their practice. Research indicates that MBSR improves focus, attention, and ability to work under stress. This book does not offer a formal MBSR plan. However, it draws on similar principles of treating mindfulness as an adventure rather than a chore, focusing on individual motivation and agency, and making the time commitment necessary to experience the benefits of mindfulness. This book can be used on its own or as a supplement to MBSR training.

The Principles of Mindfulness

The techniques and practices of mindfulness are of benefit not only to us but also to the broader world. Whatever we "practice" radiates to the people around us—family, friends, colleagues, community, and the world at large. I teach mindfulness to contribute to a better world for each individual and for the collective.

Over the years, I have found the following principles to be helpful for students to understand the nuts and bolts of mindfulness.

- **Kindness:** Some mindfulness teachers, such as Jack Kornfield, emphasize mindfulness as "kind awareness." The attention is patient, kind, warm, and respectful. Warmth of attention makes it possible to relax and be at ease. This is not possible in a judgmental environment. Kindness toward oneself and all thoughts that arise is crucial to mindfulness practice. Remember: mindfulness is not about changing anything; it is about seeing clearly what is there.

- **Curiosity:** Curiosity about what is happening in and around you is as intrinsic to mindfulness as sweetness is to sugar. Curiosity is what we mean when we talk about a "beginner's mind." The beginner's mind is open and interested without any preconceived ideas about what should be happening or what will happen. So often our assumptions or past experiences around someone or something block a true understanding of that very thing or person. To be mindful is to maintain curious attention. Watch yourself in the same way you might watch a wild animal—with curiosity, respect, and interest.

- **Non-reactivity or allowing:** Mindfulness is allowing and non-reactive. You can think of this as permission to acknowledge what you observe in yourself and what is going on around you without having to immediately take action. Mindfulness knows that "Yes, anxiety is like this," "I am really angry right now," or "In this moment, my mind is filled with painful thoughts." With mindfulness, we practice allowing whatever is here to be here. Sometimes this quality can be confusing. At some point, you might have gotten the idea that we are aiming to turn into some kind of tranquil statue that doesn't experience harsh or unpleasant feelings. That's impossible. The trick is to not engage with every thought or emotion—it's just a thought!—while allowing it to exist. You can compare this to watching clouds go by or, for city dwellers, simply observing ongoing traffic.

- **Non-striving:** There is nowhere to go and no better moment available to you than this very moment. This quality takes patience and practice. Often, when people begin their meditation practice, they find themselves striving for a peaceful moment, a less painful moment, or the moment to be different in some way. The truth about mindfulness is that it is ordinary—it does not involve optimizing or perfecting anything. The moment (and you) doesn't need to be anything other than exactly what it is.

- **Self-reliance:** Self-reliance is one of the most strengthening parts of mindfulness because it teaches us to trust and rely upon our own capacity to meet each moment—even the hard moments. This confidence is developed slowly by starting with each small moment of mindfulness. You are the authority on yourself and your experience. In learning for yourself, you'll see the great freedom and ease that arises from the practice of mindfulness.

The most important point is to accept yourself and stand on your two feet.

— *SHUNRYU SUZUKI*

Mindfulness and Meditation

Broadly speaking, meditation is any technique designed to help humans work with their experience from the inside rather than manipulating the outer world. The meditator works with their mind, emotions, and body with varied aims, such as coming into the present moment, focusing the mind, relaxing, or even increasing sleep. Some meditate to be free of suffering, to awaken to love, or to reach enlightenment. Meditation can mean different things to different people. The key is to remain awake and open to whatever you are experiencing in a specific moment in time, to relish in the temporary nature of whatever arises.

In general, meditation falls into three categories. First, there are concentration practices that focus the mind on a single object or intention, such as your breath, a candle flicker, or a specific word or phrase. Second, there are mindfulness or open awareness meditations that bring awareness to your environment, internal feelings, and bodily sensations. Third, there are "guided" meditations in which you follow the voice of a meditation teacher who usually combines elements of the prior two categories. These broad categories support each other and are often practiced in tandem.

In order to be mindful and know what is happening in the present moment, there needs to be some level of concentration or focus. You may have heard the instruction to count your breaths or repeat a phrase or word over and over (mantra). This is considered concentration practice, and it focuses the mind and supports mindfulness. However, when we practice mindfulness, we are paying attention to more than just our breath or a mantra; we are paying attention to whatever arises including, well, everything. This book includes a mixture of concentration practices, like counting breaths, and mindfulness practices, like listening to sounds. Most of the meditations and exercises include both kinds of skills and can be considered self-guided practice.

Mindfulness in a Chaotic World

The world sometimes goes through cycles that feel particularly difficult and painful. Individuals go through painful periods, too. Perhaps you have come to this book during a painful personal cycle. Or maybe situations have changed in your life, leaving you feeling uncertain, curious, searching. We all need tools to support the mind, body, and heart.

When we change our internal relationship to our experience, our life changes. Whatever it may look like to others, we are the ones living our lives, our experiences from the inside. We know best how it is to be in our bodies. Mindfulness provides clarity that allows us to see what needs to be done, whether in a single moment at home or in the broader context of the community and public affairs. When you create peace through mindfulness and meditation, it allows for harmony to flourish in a wider way—through the impact you have on your friends, family, and co-workers. When you work with mindfulness, you begin to create the world that you want to live in. You do this one moment at a time.

The next four weeks can serve as pillars for this journey. My sincere hope is that this book supports you on your exploration into mindfulness.

Laying the Foundation

Like any new skill, mindfulness is best learned through steady effort. Commitment to a regular practice is the only real way to get the habit of mindfulness to stick. That said, I have been consistently practicing mindfulness meditation for more than 20 years, and I can say for certain that the results do build even if you miss a day or two here and there (or even a month or two!). If you have lost track of your mindfulness practice, give yourself permission to start again.

As you begin to practice mindfulness, remember it is not meant to be a punishment or a grim duty. A consistent practice allows us to be more in touch with the joys and pleasures of everyday life and more compassionate with its difficulties. If you find yourself regularly dreading your mindfulness practice time, you may need to make some adjustments or seek support from a mindfulness teacher. (There are resources for finding teachers on page 167.) Resistance is a normal part of practice, but it tends to soften with time.

You can think of a daily practice for the next month as a science experiment. What happens for you if you practice daily for the next four weeks? Try to wait until the end of the month to make any sweeping evaluations. It doesn't matter if your meditation is "good" or "bad" on any one day. Simply commit to the regularity of a practice and see what you notice in your body, mind, relationships, and environment.

Growth is always a gradual process, a bridge slowly crossed and not a corner sharply turned.

— *JOHN POWELL*

Routine

It is important to establish a routine around your mindfulness practice so that you don't have to "decide" to practice every single day. Make it that much easier to practice by already knowing when you'll do it. You're a busy person, after all! When you have a routine, practice becomes a skillful habit, allowing you to become more proficient at the task at hand. A routine also provides you with the opportunity to dedicate some time to yourself for growth and healing.

I recommend a daily period of mindfulness meditation that can be anywhere from 5 to 40 minutes long. If it makes sense for you, you can also try doing two shorter practices a day (for example, five minutes in the morning and five minutes before bed). During that daily meditation, use any one of the meditations found in this book. Feel free to incorporate other resources (including phone apps) to support this journey. Although the book lays out a clear 4-week, or 28-day, plan, the goal is not to rigidly follow a program. The idea is to use the resources provided here to establish a daily routine.

Here are some tips and ideas to consider as you carve out your daily routine:

- **Time of day:** Some people find an early morning practice to be more conducive to creating a habit; others find evening practice to be easier to commit to. Find a time that works for you. Returning the same time every day requires you to think less about the "when and how," making the act of meditation more habitual and therefore easier.

- **Amount of time:** Next, pick an amount of time that works for you to commit to meditation. Five minutes per day is more impactful in establishing a lasting habit than one hour once a week. I have set the estimated meditation times for your next four weeks; you can use these as suggestions and make note of what feels like the right allotment of time for you.

- **Finding a rhythm:** Trust yourself to find a cadence and see if you can stick with it. Remember to be realistic and gentle with yourself, working within the conditions of your daily life. We are not going for unrealistically high expectations, but rather finding a way to work within your circumstances. Remember, you are experimenting, which means making adjustments along the way.

Environment

In addition to finding a consistent time and rhythm for your practice of meditation, having environmental cues can be a helpful way to maintain your practice. Some people like to have a place set aside or some particular objects as part of the environment for meditation. If you are fortunate enough to have a space that you can dedicate, do your best to remove excess clutter and distractions.

Even if you don't have a designated area in your home, perhaps you have an object or two that reminds you of your intentions to practice mindfulness. This can include a diffuser, a plant, a rug or meditation pillow, a stone, a poem, or a picture that calms you. There is no right or wrong way to create a peaceful environment for *you*.

Although it can be a necessary part of life to engage with electronic devices, for the brief moment of mindfulness practice, see if you can follow these guidelines:

- No screens

- No alarms

- No buzzing

If you want to use your phone as a timer, I recommend turning on airplane mode. You can also flip it over so the light won't catch your eye and take you out of your meditation. Although these recommendations might seem detail oriented, it's these small acts of intentionality that make the difference in our practice.

Intention

What brought you to your mindfulness practice? It is helpful to remember why you are doing something so that when it gets difficult or doesn't turn out the way you think that it should, you know why you are hanging in there. Intentions are powerful because your mind is powerful. Set an intention at the start of each exercise or meditation that you do. Here are some example intentions:

- Inner peace

- Staying present

- Practicing self-kindness

- Finding gratitude for the self or a specific individual

- Bringing awareness to feelings

- Supporting health

- Enhancing focus

The possibilities are endless! Be creative and sincere and you can't go wrong. Let your intention support you in the effort to have a daily practice, and when you encounter resistance, remember your intention so that it can support you.

Mantras

The word "mantra" comes from the Sanskrit word *man*, meaning "mind," and *tra*, meaning "vehicle" or "instrument." Literally a "vehicle for the mind," a mantra is a phrase or word you can use to concentrate the mind during meditation. It is a technique that takes you from distraction to focus. Mantras are found across the globe and appear in many religions (think of the rosary practice in Catholicism). You can pick an English or Sanskrit word or phrase and say your mantra daily or repeat it during a meditation. For example, if you pick "peace," say the word gently in your mind with each breath and invite the feeling of peace at the same time.

Posture

During a formal meditation practice, your posture matters because posture both reflects and influences your thinking mind, mood, and emotional space. With posture, as we will also see with breath, the mind and body are intimately intertwined. (Try slumping in an exaggerated way and see what comes up in your mind. Conversely, sit up straight and notice how you feel.)

As best as you can while meditating, lengthen along the spine. Keep in mind that your spine should be lengthened without you having to make too much effort. You can use support for this. If you are sitting on the ground, put pillows under your hips to help the alignment in the pelvis and therefore the spine. If you are sitting in a chair, consider putting a thin pillow behind you and along the spine so that the spine does not round or slump. Let your body find a posture that feels supported and at ease within the conditions of your body in the present moment.

Keep in mind: You do not have to sit on the floor or on a pillow to meditate. Meditation can be done sitting, standing, reclining, or walking. The key is to find a position where your body feels supported and can stay relatively still. Find a posture that works for the body that you have; this can and does include lying down or standing up.

Breath

The breath is a powerful tool, in mindfulness practice and in life. The more you become aware of the ability of your breath to calm your body and regulate your mind, the easier it will become to start applying this tool to all aspects of your life. You take your breath everywhere you go, and it is always there to support you.

In any given moment, there are a myriad of things happening. Therefore, when practicing mindfulness, we must decide where to direct our attention. For millennia, humans have turned to the breath as this primary place of attention. Placing attention on the breath focuses the mind even as other things such as bodily sensations, sounds, thoughts, and emotions arise and pass.

When you meditate with the breath as the primary object of attention, you are not thinking about the breath. The technique is to feel the sensations of the movement of the breath in real time rather than to think about the breath itself. Please note that the breath is not the only object of attention that can be used while practicing mindfulness. One can also choose to use a mantra, sounds, or bodily sensations as a primary place for attention. (Most of the exercises and meditations in this book use the breath as the primary object.)

The breath is a useful primary object of attention for three reasons:

1. **It's constant:** The breath is always active, a continuous, repeating pattern of sensation. It is easier to pay attention to something that is both consistent and changing.

2. **It's neutral:** This means it is not a painful sensation for most people. It is easier to pay

attention without fatigue or reactivity to something that does not hurt.

3. **It's both ordinary and spectacular:** Breath supports the fire of your life and embeds you in the greater world. Our inhale is dependent on the oxygen in the atmosphere, and the plants are dependent on our exhale. The breath is with you from birth to death, and it is a symbol of our symbiosis with the natural world.

In mindfulness practice, you do not need to manipulate your breath to feel its grounding effect; instead, you can allow it to be spontaneous. It may be short or long, shallow or deep. While practicing mindfulness, as best as you can, allow the breath to be spontaneous and natural.

It's worth noting, though, that in some yoga traditions, the breath is altered for desired outcomes, such as calming the nervous system or conversely raising vitality and energy. Later in your practice, on Day 17, you will manipulate the breath in order to help calm the autonomic nervous system. This conscious breathing signals to your body that you are safe, you can relax, and you can slow down.

Allowing the breath to be natural can be challenging for many reasons. You might be used to controlling it in yoga, you might have asthma or a cold, you might be subconsciously using the breath to manage emotions or experience, or you might have never thought to be aware of it at all. All of these are common and a normal part of this process.

At the beginning of each exercise and meditation, I ask you to take three clearing breaths. This is a small ritual to let your mind and heart know that you are entering your mindfulness practice. It is also an opportunity to let go of whatever has been happening, because the breath can be an incredibly useful aid in letting go. Finally, the deeper, slower breathing pattern is calming for the autonomic nervous system.

Reflection

Mindfulness allows us to see more clearly into the rich tapestry of our lives. For some people, it can also open up a flow of creative ideas or insights into life, problems, and relationships. For this reason, many people find it helpful to bring a pen to page after a meditation to capture some of their ideas and insights. Others find it helpful to note the general flow of what happened during the practice in order to track patterns and sharpen awareness. Writing is another way you can build the habit of mindfulness.

However, during meditation it is important to keep meditating instead of stopping to write something down. As best you can, refrain from writing during the meditation and instead keep coming back to the present moment so that a new thought or new experience can arise. (The brilliant ones will resurface again after the meditation, too!)

Some prompts for reflection after meditation include:

- What was a general theme?

- If my body could talk, what would it say?

- What is really true for me right now?

- What is my intention for the day?

- What am I grateful for?

Your First Meditation Prep

Remember that mindfulness is the process of purposefully noticing what is happening in the present moment without judgment. Meditation provides us an undisturbed amount of time to practice doing this.

Often the first thing that people notice when meditating is that the mind is full of thoughts.

Thinking is a habit we all possess—it makes sense that when we sit down to meditate, we notice thoughts bubbling up. Just as it is the natural function of the stomach to digest, it is the natural function of the mind to think. We cannot stop thoughts, but we can choose how to engage with them. As a matter of course, thoughts are not a problem during meditation. We can notice thoughts in the same way that we notice sounds or sensations. However, our thoughts can cause us pain or frustration when they become very loud or stuck in a loop.

Because thinking is habitual, it is hard to stop thoughts in any one moment. However, through mindfulness, we can begin to relate to them in a different way that allows them to slow and become more workable. When we create distance from our thoughts, we realize every thought is just that—a thought. It is not reality. For example, your thought about your friend is not the same as your friend. In general, the less you try to make your thoughts go away, the easier it is to deal with them and see the bigger reality. I find it helpful to thank my brain for its thoughts as I become aware of them. Other people find it helpful to place their thoughts in front or to the left of them. They're your thoughts, and you decide exactly how to engage with them. So how, then, does meditation come in?

Meditation is an openness to wherever you (and your thoughts) are in the moment. Especially at the beginning of our mindfulness journey, it is easy to be judgmental or performative about the act of meditation itself or to wonder things like "Am I doing it right?"

Mindfulness is an invitation to get out of that entire frame of mind and instead just be with yourself, whatever is happening. This is why I talk about meditation as a "practice," not a "perfect." It doesn't matter if you didn't feel peaceful or had a restless mind. The idea is to just do it and trust that the effort itself is enough.

There are no grades, no awards for being a better breather. (In fact, I am pretty sure that you are a great breather.) Let yourself practice with as little judgment as you can muster and see what happens. What might your life look like if you let go for a brief moment and stopped trying to optimize everything? Is it possible to enjoy even the imperfections? Another way to say this is: enjoy the perfectly imperfect, wild ride of the human spirit.

Foundational Meditation

5 minutes

In this first meditation, you are building the skills of mindfulness and focus. You'll begin by noticing what is happening inside your body and what arises as your mind tries to settle with mindfulness. You'll also hone the central focusing skill of coming back to the breath.

- Find a posture that is relaxed and at ease. You can sit on the floor or in a chair, or you may lie down.
- You may leave your eyes open or closed. (If you recline, keep your eyes open.) If your eyes are open, keep the gaze soft and down.
- Take three big, slow breaths in and out through the nose. Each time, inhale fully and then exhale slowly.
- Set your intention for your meditation.
- Start at the top of your head and slowly work your way down your entire body, relaxing what is easy to relax as you go. Do this for about two minutes.
- Bring your attention to the feeling of the breath at your upper belly. Notice the

sensations of movement as you breathe. (Note: Don't think about the breath. Instead, just feel the movements as they happen.)

- Continue noticing the sensations of the breath at your belly until something else arises, whether it is a thought, sound, sensation in your body, or emotion. Anything can happen! When you notice something else besides the breath, make a note of that. For example, you can make a quiet mental note that "Sound is happening," or "Anxiety is like this."

- When the mind wanders, notice that you have been thinking, and thank your mind for its thoughts. Bring your attention gently and slowly back to the feeling of the breath.

- When you are finished, make a small bow to acknowledge the sincerity of your effort.

Adjustment

For some, feeling the breath at the belly is uncomfortable or just doesn't work. You are welcome to change where you feel the sensations of the breath. The attention to breath sensations can also be placed at the nose or the ribs. Pick one place and stick to it for a while.

You can practice this meditation any time of the day or night. It will help support your daily mindfulness practice and be a welcome place to return to, again and again.

Mindfulness in the Body

Mindfulness is centered in the body—its movements, pains, and strength are the bedrock of practicing mindfulness. Diving deeper into the wisdom of the body is the first, and arguably the deepest, foundation of mindfulness. That's right: To better understand the mind, we expand our awareness of the body. It's for this reason that this four-week plan begins with a return home to the body where you breathe, walk, run, dance, play, eat, sleep, and exist.

The body is always in the present moment, whether it is sleepy, joyful, hungry, angry—you name it. You experience your life not just in your mind, but through your body. It is your intimate connection with the world around you and the way you inhabit it. The body is water, the same chemical compound that flows in the rivers and oceans. Your breath is the atmosphere taken into your bloodstream. The hardness of your bones is found in the minerals in the soil. Your aliveness energy is the energy of the sun transformed into you.

This extends to the ways we use our bodies, too. You touch a friend with your hand, hold a child with your arms, enjoy a meal with your family. Your entire life happens with and through your body. Rage rips through, anxiety quivers, and joy bubbles. Peace can be felt like a soothing balm through the heart.

Yet the concept of mindfulness can run counter to cultural or clinical messages to view our bodies as objects to be controlled, manipulated, or maintained. Mindfulness asks us to feel and inhabit ourselves from the inside out, developing a deeply respectful and kind relationship to our physical form. This is a powerful place to be: living from the inside of your body rather than from a place of external shame, judgment, or simple disregard.

One key to mindfulness practice involves getting more in tune with the moment-to-moment experience of our bodies. Can you notice your body right now, the one you have today—not the one anyone else tells you that you should have? Can you feel the aliveness of your body right now? Notice your hands, shoulders, belly, knees. What do you notice?

The exercises this week focus on getting more in tune with and going into the body. This can be an intense experience if we are not used to this level of awareness, yet all it really consists of is a return home. You may have a difficult relationship with your body, you might take detailed care of your corpus, or you may have never thought about it much at all. When we slow down enough to actually inhabit the body, it becomes a new source of knowledge, giving us information about what we are feeling and where we might be storing things. Instead of our ideas or fantasies about our body, we can have authentic, just-right-now experiences in our body. These practices will help you create and maintain a healthy relationship with your body and wake up into the aliveness that is your birthright.

The next week of mindfulness meditations and exercises centered on the body will help you:

- Stay present and grounded in the moment

- Inhabit the body, a place of power

- Build a healthy foundation of knowledge around *your* body

- Support your overall health

- Develop deeper body wisdom and compassion

You can always come back to these exercises as a touchstone to deepen your experience with your body and strengthen your practice of mindfulness.

Mindfulness isn't just about knowing that you're hearing something, seeing something, or even observing that you're having a particular feeling. It's about doing so in a certain way—with balance and equanimity, and without judgment. Mindfulness is the practice of paying attention in a way that creates space for insight.

— SHARON SALZBERG

Day 1: Body Scan

5 minutes

A body scan is a powerful mindfulness exercise designed to help you feel and inhabit your body from the inside, bringing kind awareness to your body, part by part. A body scan can temper anxiety or other overwhelming emotions and teach you to ride the wave of whatever is happening in the moment. Although the body scan is a beginning mindfulness practice, don't be fooled into thinking that you need to "advance" past it. You can return to it again and again.

- There are many different ways to do this type of meditation, so feel free to experiment. In general, the idea is to bring attention to each part of the body in a systematic way. The pace of attention to each part is not too slow or fast.
- Find a comfortable position with a lengthened spine, sitting, standing, or reclining.
- Remember your specific intention or a general one of goodwill for yourself.
- Take three slow, clearing breaths.
- Start at the very crown of your head, noticing your scalp. Remain open to any sensations; spend a few moments here.
- Move down slowly, incrementally bringing awareness to the front, sides, and back of your head. Spend a few moments in each spot, allowing time for sensations to appear. This will create a "ring" of sensation.
- Continue moving down your body in rings. Spend longer on any areas that seem tight, painful, or interesting. Notice if there are areas that get skipped.
- Once you get to the bottom of the feet, if you have time, complete the same sequence again.
- Make a small bow with folded hands to finish.

Challenge

You may nod off and find yourself coming back to awareness. Or the mind may wander, and you may lose track of where you are or even what you are doing. When that happens, thank your mind for its thoughts! Tell your mind that you will get back to the thoughts later, and just start the whole procedure again from the top of your head. Don't worry if you have to start over many times. Starting over is like doing reps at the gym. If done without judgment, starting over increases the strength of the mind.

Adjustment

If you are experiencing pain that makes it difficult to focus, you can try these two different modifications. First, try spending a little more time with the painful area. This may sound counterintuitive, but give it a try for the sake of experimentation. Breathe into the pain while letting go of the idea that it is pain. Instead, notice the details of the sensations. What specifically is happening? Is the sensation hot or cold? Achy and throbbing or sharp and intense? What does the area adjacent to the pain feel like? Do the sensations shift? Sometimes when moving attention closer to pain, we find that the pain becomes more bearable, shifts, or even disappears. The second modification that can be helpful is to spend more time focusing on areas that feel okay-to-good as a respite from intense sensation. (We will talk further about pain on Day 7 [see page 62.])

Day 2: Walking Now

15–20 minutes

For many people, walking is a daily activity they don't think that much about. Yet walking is a great time to practice mindfulness (put that phone away!), as we are often on our own out in the world. Walking doesn't require much else besides our bodies, but it provides a great opportunity to fully enter the present moment. You can think about this meditation as less about going for a walk than practicing mindfulness as an exercise while walking.

Increasing awareness of the present moment, our bodily sensations, and our thoughts on our daily walks—any time we walk from A to B—allows us to incorporate mindfulness into our lives throughout the day in a seamless way.

- Decide where you would like to walk. This can be indoors or outside. You will need a spot that is about 10 to 20 strides long.
- Stand and set your intention to be present while walking.
- Take three clearing breaths.
- Notice that you are standing by sensing your feet, legs, spine, and torso.
- Take a step and feel the sensations from your feet and legs.
- Walk 10 to 20 additional paces while noticing the sensations in the feet and legs. Find a pace that feels just right for paying attention to the sensations in your feet and legs, anywhere from very slow to brisk.
- When you get to the end of your walking area, stop. Bring your awareness to your feet, legs, spine, and torso.

- Turn around, noticing the sensations in the feet, legs, and hips as you turn around.
- Walk back to your starting place, aware of the changing sensations in your toes, feet, legs, and spine.
- Stop when you are back at the beginning spot. Simply take note that you are standing.
- Turn around and repeat the sequence as many times as you like.
- Allow the pace to adjust itself.
- When you are finished, make a small bow with folded hands, or reach down to touch the Earth.

Challenge

Some people say they feel bored when meditating. If this happens to you, try to notice what boredom feels like and continue with the process. Do you experience boredom somewhere in your body? Let it be a teacher to deepen the lesson. Resist the urge to walk backwards or entertain yourself with fancy walking. Embrace the boredom! Continue the exercise for the amount of time that you decided, and see if something shifts or changes with your thoughts, emotions, or body.

Adjustment

If you have limited walking ability or range of motion, there are simple adjustments you can make to achieve the same end. The important part of this meditation is to move the body in a rhythmic and repetitive way while paying attention to bodily sensations. For example, you can do this exercise with attention to your shoulders and hips as you swim or walk in a pool. Another way to practice would be to experiment with lifting and lowering your arms, one at a time in a repetitive fashion, while paying attention to sensations in your arms. Feel free to be creative!

Day 3: Floating in the Present

5–10 minutes

Mindfulness can be practiced seated, standing, walking, or lying down. That is to say, it can be practiced in any posture. I teach meditation in both seated and reclining positions. In general, people love the relaxed benefits of reclining meditation, but some express concern that they feel like it is not the "real thing"—that they are somehow cheating. This is a common concern, but you can let that judgment float on by.

Reclining meditations can have surprising benefits, including relieving pain from the seated position. By lying down, one can learn how to deeply be at ease. While seated, many people have the tendency to overexert in the meditation. This position is great to counterbalance that. Most importantly, deliberate, conscious rest combined with a structured mindfulness practice leads to a natural vitality and aliveness.

- Turn off your phone and any other electronic devices. You can set an alarm if you need to get up at the end of the meditation.
- Find a quiet place to lie down, and make yourself comfortable with a thin pillow under your head and possibly a cushion or blanket under your knees. You may also want to cover yourself with a blanket. Remember that your intention is to rest with kind, mindful attention.
- Feel free to close your eyes.
- Take three deep, cleansing breaths.
- Start by flexing and moving your hands. Then, allow them to relax.
- Take a few moments to feel your hands and fingers. Notice the temperature and weight of your hands, as well as any tingling or pulsation.

- Next, move to your feet. Wiggle your toes and circle the ankles. Notice any sensations. Take your time and allow the sensations to arise spontaneously.
- Move your attention from the bottom of your body slowly to the top. Relax what is easy to relax as you go. Finally, squeeze and tighten your face like you have just eaten a lemon, then let it relax. Remain open to any sensations from your face for a few minutes.
- When you are finished, take one slow breath.
- Rest for a few seconds with your eyes open before sitting up.

Challenge

You might fall asleep! Please don't worry if this happens; your body might be needing a little more sleep. You can just try this meditation again at another time. With practice, you will learn to stay awake.

Adjustment

Try this meditation with open eyes and a soft gaze to help your attention stay alert and focused. You can also practice it sitting up in a comfortable chair if reclining is not available to you.

Let everything happen to you:

Beauty and terror.

Just keep going.

No feeling is final.

— *RAINER MARIA RILKE*

Day 4: Whole-Body Breathing

5–10 minutes

On Day 4, we will be doing something new. Instead of a sharp and laser-like focus on a single part of the body, whether it is the breath or an actual body part, today we work with attention in a broader way in order to feel the body from the inside all at once. In other words, we will drop out of the conceptual mind and into the experience of the totality of the body. To do this, I give an instruction that is more poetic than rational or scientific: Breathe with your whole body—not just with your nose or lungs, but as if your whole body could respire.

Sometimes people find it easier to start small by trying this with a hand. Wiggle your fingers and move them around. Then, close your eyes and instead of seeing your hand in your mind's eye, put the attention into sensations of your hand. Imagine your hand taking a big breath as if the skin were porous, and you could actually feel the air moving through it. Experiment to see what works for you. When shifting to the entire body, some people find it helpful to imagine that the skin on their whole body is porous and that the breath can somehow move in and out of everywhere at once. Or maybe you feel the breath as you simultaneously feel the entire body at once, like you have a wide-angle lens on all of the sensations of your posture and breath.

Use your intuition and work in a way that makes sense to you rather than making an effort to try to get it right. Remember that staying with the practice is an investment in yourself and your well-being. Working in different ways allows us to keep a flexible and responsive mind.

- Find a comfortable and steady posture, seated or lying down.
- Remember your intention for your mindfulness practice.
- Take three deep clearing breaths.
- Spend a little bit of time relaxing your body.
- Notice your whole body as you breathe. It is as if the entire body is receiving the oxygen on the inhale and letting go of carbon dioxide on the exhale.
- When something arises, whether it is a thought, sound, emotion, or sensation, notice what is happening. Allow everything that arises to be like clouds passing through the sky. Do not judge the clouds or anything that arises.
- Breathe with your whole body as you feel the entire body in its posture. It is as if the vitality of the breath could move through your entire

body at once. Don't leave any part of your body out. Feel your torso, arms, legs, and head as you breathe.

- When you are finished, take a small bow with folded hands.

Challenge

This meditation might be difficult, as the attention is broad. You may find it helpful to have a sense of the space both inside and outside of your body. Watch out for trying to "do it right"—whatever method works for you, embrace it. (It's a good thing to evolve from guided instruction!) If you find this one difficult, don't give up right away; allow time to get acclimated.

Adjustment

If breathing is difficult, or it is taking too much effort, try lying down. Of course, you can do any of the meditations while lying down, but this meditation in particular can be really lovely while reclining so that you do not make too much unnecessary effort.

Turn your wounds into wisdom.

— OPRAH WINFREY

Day 5: Body Benevolence

15 minutes

Your body goes everywhere with you. The list of what it does for you is long: Your stomach digests your food, your heart keeps your blood flowing, etc. Your fingernails are growing right now. Your body shows up whether it has gotten enough (or too much) sleep or eaten a healthy and fulfilling meal. Mindfulness of your body creates conditions for a more respectful and loving relationship with it, no matter how or where it moves through the world. Sometimes it helps to use a targeted practice to cultivate a kind relationship with the body.

Today's exercise is designed to specifically help with the cultivation of a kind and compassionate attitude toward the body. We always start where we are and, from there, work toward growth and compassion. No matter what your relationship to your body is, you can offer more and more love toward it. The result? Ease in relationship to your body.

- Find a comfortable position in a place where you can practice undisturbed.
- Set an intention to cultivate benevolence for your body.
- Take three clearing breaths.

- Start by bringing your attention to your hands. You can wiggle them or squeeze and extend them.
- Let the hands rest down on your body. Take a few moments to allow the sensations in the hands to become clear.
- Reflect on all that your hands do for you. They help you communicate, they touch your loved ones, they feed you, they scratch your itches.
- Continue feeling your hands. Let the attention be imbued with appreciation and benevolence.
- Next, move to your neck and throat. Feel free to move your neck, shoulders, and jaw.
- Take a few moments to allow any sensations to arise from your neck and throat.
- Reflect on all that your neck and throat do for you. The neck holds up your head, which is no small feat! It allows your head to look from side to side. Your throat sings and laughs and cries. Your food travels down it.
- Continue feeling this area with attention. Allow the attention to be a kind, gentle, and healing touch.
- Move to any other body parts, such as your belly or feet, that you would like to explore.

Offer those body parts benevolence and gratitude. Take your time.

- When you are finished, take a moment to thank your body for all that it does for you.

Challenge

Sometimes the thinking mind gets carried away with the directed thoughts of all that a body part does for you. Then the mind takes off into other stories and thought streams. If this happens, skip this part. Instead, focus on breathing through the part of the body that you are working with, and imagine that the breath is filled with benevolence.

Adjustment

This meditation can bring up resistance. Sometimes feelings that are very much the opposite of benevolence, kindness, and compassion can flood through you. Be patient with yourself. Other times a kind of disconnection and lack of feeling can arise. Nothing that arises is wrong, and no feeling is lasting. Part of the way that mindfulness allows us to come back into healthy alignment is by giving us the space to experience something, then let it go. Go slow, take your time, and revisit this exercise to see what changes happen with repeated efforts.

You do not have to be good.

You do not have to walk on your knees

for a hundred miles through the desert repenting.

You only have to let the soft animal of your body

love what it loves.

— *MARY OLIVER*

Day 6: A Mindful Morsel

10 minutes

On Day 6 of your first week of mindfulness practice, we'll turn to mindful eating, or bringing our awareness to the process of putting food in our bodies. The first time I tried mindful eating, my relationship to food that I thought I disliked changed. It turns out that some of the foods that I thought I disliked just weren't as pleasurable as my "favorite" foods. Isn't that curious? Something that I had thought was set—my dislike of mushrooms—was actually not quite certain. Things change, people change. It can be freeing to be a new person—someone who doesn't mind mushrooms!

But mindful eating is about more than just what we like and dislike. We eat for pleasure, comfort, taste, health, habit, and survival. Even a small snack connects us to the sun, rain, air, and soil from which food originates. Eating food is one of the most poignant and everyday ways we experience our connection to Earth and its rhythms, cycles, and seasons, as well as to the broad community of people across the Earth on whom we are dependent to cultivate and supply us with food. We could not live without all of these relationships. This is the essence of interdependence.

The following exercise brings kind awareness to the elemental act of nourishing ourselves. This exercise is to be practiced with a spirit of renewal and care. The main idea is to eat with as much curiosity and interest as possible. It does not matter what you eat, how you eat, or when you eat. The exercise is just to know that you are eating and respectfully notice whatever arises.

- Set some time aside to eat alone or in the company of someone who is interested in eating silently and mindfully with you.
- Turn off your phone and any other electronic devices. Embark on this meditation in silence if possible.
- Sit down with your food in front of you, and remember your intention to eat with kindness and curiosity.
- Take three clearing breaths. Notice your body in the chair and the food in front of you.
- Then, notice if you are hungry. If you are hungry, what are the physical sensations of hunger?
- If you want to, you can include a brief moment of reflection to express gratitude for the food, where it came from, the seasons it took to

grow, and the people who cultivated, transported, and sold it.

- Then, begin to eat. Notice the taste and texture of the food. Is it pleasurable? Notice the actions of chewing and swallowing.
- Bring your awareness to any sounds you hear, and note if you find them pleasant, unpleasant, or neutral.
- If you are drinking something, notice the texture of the liquid.
- Note the sensations from your stomach as the meal continues. When you feel finished, what feels "finished"? Are you satiated or would you like more?
- Practice noticing like an interested scientist, without any idea of how the experiment will end. You can even notice thoughts and judgments. Once you are done, pause and note that you have finished before clearing things away.
- You also may find it helpful to write some reflections about what you discovered.

Challenge

Remember this exercise is not meant to change your relationship to any one food or pattern but instead to offer the conditions to bring more kindness, sensation, and gratitude into each snack or meal. If your mind starts to wander, pause and then start again. (Warning: Try not to force this exercise on reluctant friends or family members! They will explore this process when and if they are ready.)

Adjustment

Due to life's many conditions, it can be difficult to find the space to have a whole meal in silence. Feel free to take the pause at the beginning of this exercise before you eat, or just take a few bites with kind attention. Since eating is so much a part of our day-to-day lives, both on our own or with others, opportunities for bringing this kind attention to our eating are very accessible.

Day 7: Touching Pain

10 minutes

You've made it to the final day of the first week of instruction. How does your body feel? Are you finding yourself more situated in or at least aware of your bones? As we shift to Day 7, we turn to the experience of pain in the body. People experience pain in many different ways. Often the experience of pain is colored by an emotional response. Mindfulness has been shown to help people manage pain as well as reduce emotional reactions to pain.

One of my favorite parts of being a yoga teacher is hearing about everyone's physical injuries, illness, and pain. I like hearing people's stories because it reminds me that everyone has a body that is subject to pain, illness, and injury, and we share this experience in our common humanity. Pain is one of the most common and human things we can experience. (I get migraines and have had some chronic pain. What do you experience?)

Yet in this very human experience, we can also carry so much shame and fear. Thoughts like "If I had only done ____, I wouldn't be feeling this," or "What did I do to deserve this?" might arise. We might also look around and think that everyone else has everything in working order. Through mindfulness practice, we can create a new relationship to pain, one free from shame and blame. Pain can be an opportunity for compassion to grow as we see that it is not so personal, but a universal human experience.

Remember: Mindfulness is imbued with kindness. This is doubly more important when dealing with something difficult like pain. You might consider working first with pain that is less intense to build up those mindfulness "muscles."

- Find a comfortable, quiet place to practice this exercise.
- Place one hand on the center of your chest, then stack the other hand on top of that. Remind yourself of your intention to support yourself through something difficult like pain.
- Your hands can stay where they are or rest wherever is comfortable.
- Take three clearing breaths.
- Remember that pain is part of being human; others feel pain too. Also remember that pain is not your fault.
- Spend as long as you would like practicing mindfulness of the breath to steady your mind and heart.

- When you feel ready, bring your attention to a painful sensation. Get really close to the sensations of pain without going into thoughts or analysis about the situation. Just feel the sensations as closely and as accurately as possible.

- Do the sensations move, shift, or change? Do they have a texture or temperature? Are they stabbing, pulsing, or steady? What happens as you again and again bring your attention to the pain? Stay here for as long as you would like. Note that getting close to painful sensations can lead to reactivity and an unsustainable intensity. If this happens, move your attention to an adjacent area that is not feeling pain.

- Notice if any stories or emotions arise. You can name the experience: "Stories are like this," or "Anger is like this."

- When you are finished exploring the painful sensations, move the attention to another part of your body that feels okay or even pleasant. Let your attention rest in this new place. It doesn't have to be a big area; it could be your pinky toenail. Let your mind refresh itself in the restfulness of that spot. Breathe here naturally for a few minutes or as long as you would like.

- Place your hands on your heart whenever you need additional support.
- Return to mindfulness of the breath.
- To finish, make a small bow to acknowledge your efforts.

Challenge

This exercise is not meant to make the pain go away but instead to help us offer kindness and support. It can be helpful to treat yourself like you would a close friend who is having difficulty rather than falling into judgment. It is not a failure to find this exercise to be too much. Yet continuing to practice helps build steadiness and a trust in yourself and your body. Working with pain is an art unto itself.

Adjustment

You can return to the other meditations and exercises if you find them more helpful than diving directly into the sensations of pain.

You think your pain and your heartbreak are unprecedented in the history of the world . . . The things that tormented me most were the very things that connected me with all the people who were alive, or who had ever been alive.

— *JAMES BALDWIN*

Mindfulness at Home

The first week anchored you in the present moment through your body. You are now ready to bring the skill of mindfulness of the body into your home life.

The home is a place where we nurture and take care of physical needs, such as sustenance, sleep, and hygiene. For many, home is a place of physical shelter as well as where we work. For the fortunate, it is a place of emotional refuge. Whatever and wherever your home environment is, the following chapter will support you in the cultivation of the habit of mindfulness.

In this chapter, we start to see how mindfulness can be expanded from formal seated (or walking), timed meditations into daily tasks. The exercises here bring mindfulness into your home routines, such as brushing your teeth, doing the dishes, and taking care of those in your household, including pets.

You'll also experience meditations that inspire emotional observation and reflection to support your internal experience as you go through the ups and downs—the comfort and conflict—of home life. Thought and emotion are powerful forces in a human life, and mindfulness creates the conditions necessary for a more balanced and compassionate relationship with them both. The week ends with a gratitude practice to deepen awareness of the many gifts of life.

By the end of this week, you will be able to better:

- Integrate mindfulness into basic routines like simple chores and personal hygiene.

- Explore your relationship to thought and emotion.

- Deepen your experience and facility with mindfulness as it relates to your home.

- Find gratitude in the everyday.

This being human is a guest house.
Every morning a new arrival.

A joy, a depression, a meanness,
some momentary awareness comes
as an unexpected visitor.

Welcome and entertain them all!
Even if they're a crowd of sorrows,
who violently sweep your house
empty of its furniture,
still, treat each guest honorably.
He may be clearing you out
for some new delight.

The dark thought, the shame, the malice.
meet them at the door laughing,
and invite them in.

Be grateful for whoever comes,
because each has been sent
as a guide from beyond.

— *JALALUDDIN RUMI*

Day 8: Brushing with Attention

2–3 minutes

You probably brush your teeth twice a day without thinking about it much. It is, however, a habitual act of care for your health. Because it's already a habitual activity, it is a great way to concurrently layer in your regular mindfulness practice.

- Take three clearing breaths.
- Notice that you are about to brush your teeth; run your tongue across your top and bottom teeth, suck in the sides of your cheeks, stick out your tongue several times. You are activating the awareness of your mouth.
- Now, pay close attention to the bristles of your brush, the handle of the toothpaste; watch the running water, maybe placing a hand under it.
- As you bring the toothbrush closer to your mouth, notice the smell of the toothpaste. Finally, experience the taste!
- Stay connected to the feeling of your feet and legs as you begin to brush.

- Keep bringing your attention back to the sensations of brushing your teeth. What do your gums feel like? Do you find that your tongue follows the brush wherever it goes?
- Note any thoughts or emotions and come back to the task at hand.
- When you are finished, acknowledge that you have done a simple act of care for your health.

Challenge

Perhaps you have a hard time standing still while you brush your teeth. This can be worked with in two different ways. First, "make" yourself stand still. Try holding onto the sink! You can bring mindfulness to the sensations of wanting to move without having to act on them. Second, stand on one foot while you brush. Observe the sensations of standing on one foot. Try both legs. This method has the added benefit of building your balancing skills, which decline as we age.

Adjustment

Try mindfulness with any routine hygiene task. Perhaps you wash your face daily. Bring attention to the feeling of the washcloth and the water. Hear the sounds of water and feel the texture of the towel when you dry your face. What fresh perspective can you bring to these mundane tasks of life?

Day 9: Fullness of the Moment

2–5 minutes

I have such fond memories of going for hikes with a close friend and her little one. We would sing to the baby in the car on the way to the hike and push her in the stroller up the hills over the ocean. This seems like it happened just yesterday, but the little one just had her eighteenth birthday! Life, with or without children, goes so fast, and we all have so much we feel we must get done. Mindfulness is about cultivating real-time awareness so we do not miss our lives in the midst of this flurry.

The following exercise is designed to help you take in the fullness of any specific moment in time. This applies to any and everything you might encounter in your home life. It is a pause so that you can savor the moment without any pressure to do anything; it is an invitation into the fullness and immediacy of any moment in your life.

This exercise can be done whenever you remember your intention to practice mindfulness. At that point, just take a pause. If you can, sit down and take one breath. If possible, close your eyes. See how many things you can notice, first externally and then internally; the idea is to completely expand your awareness. Start with the external environment and notice sounds around you. It might be a cacophony! Then any smells. Nothing is to be left out.

If your eyes are open, notice that you are seeing. Begin to bring your attention inward by noticing the touch and temperature of the air on your skin. Bring awareness to the position that your body is in, whether sitting or standing. Notice and connect with the feeling of your weight being supported by the chair or the floor under your feet. Notice any body pain. Notice any emotions. When you are ready, just return to doing what you had been previously doing.

Challenge

What if you are grumpy or angry, sad or hungry? If we have overwhelming emotions that are related to another person or situation, it can be challenging to stay with ourselves and our own feelings rather than spilling them, often unskillfully, onto others. This exercise is about being with the fullness of the moment without drawing others in. If you find yourself wanting to engage with others, see if you can take another breath (or five) and finish this particular exercise before engaging with anyone. You can also explore the meditation on emotions (see page 88) or speech (see page 114).

Adjustment

If you have people around you needing your immediate attention, you can shorten this exercise to a second or two. Just one breath, taking note of your surroundings, can sometimes be enough to sense the fullness of a moment.

The best and most beautiful things in the world cannot be seen nor even touched, but just felt in the heart.

— *HELEN KELLER*

Day 10: At One with the Dishes

10–15 minutes

My partner has a poster by an American cartoonist, R. Crumb, of a popular character named Mr. Natural doing dishes. Mr. Natural starts off very grumpy because of the big pile of dishes, but he ends up happy when he is finished and declares, "Another job well done." Many of us have strong feelings, either positive or negative, about simple tasks such as doing dishes. Personally, I feel grumpy like Mr. Natural when I have to do dishes. Yet mindfulness during even these simple (and sometimes arduous) tasks allows us to forgo our underlying opinions about them and drop into the direct experience of the task.

When you are ready to clean some dishes, pause for just a brief moment. Take one breath and remember your intention to cultivate the habit of mindfulness while doing the dishes. You'll do this by immersing yourself in your senses as you do this chore. When you start, notice the sensations of your feet and legs. Hear the sound of the running water, smell the dish soap, and feel the water on your hands. Slow down just a little in order to see how many different things you can sense and feel directly through your body. Textures may become more vivid. Your mind may wander; if it does, just notice what you are thinking about, like a kind friend listening. (You can even thank your mind for the glorious gift of thought!) Redirect your attention back to the fullness of the physical sensations of doing the dishes. When you have finished, make a mental note of finishing. Observe the shift in the environment. Notice if there is a shift in your own experience.

Challenge

Sometimes during your practice others may be around needing attention or wanting to talk. We can practice mindfulness while doing more than one thing at a time, but early on in your practice, this exercise will be easier if you are alone. Try to wait for opportunities to do this on your own the first few times you try.

Adjustment

This exercise is not limited to dishes. Try it with any household chore, such as vacuuming, making the bed, taking out the garbage, or doing the laundry.

Day 11: Mantra Medicine

10 minutes

The untamed or untrained mind is sometimes referred to as the "monkey mind." Often, the mind is like a monkey swinging from branch to branch, hopping from thought to thought with seemingly no sense of reason or clarity. A mantra practice can help the mind settle down. Today, you will work with the mantra "OM."

OM is a mantra from ancient Hindu, Buddhist, and Jain practices. It is said that all of creation arises from the sound of OM. It represents the entirety of the universe, both known and unknown. When working with mantra, traditionally the mantra will first be chanted or spoken aloud, then whispered, and finally transferred into a mental sound. Try chanting or toning the sound OM. It is not quite correct to call it singing, as staying in tune and sounding "good" are not important. The important part is to feel the vibration of the sound.

- Find a seat somewhere quiet with no distractions.
- Remember your intention to calm the monkey mind.
- Take three clearing breaths.
- As you breathe out, "sing" or tone the sound OM for the entire length of the exhale.
- Feel the vibration of the sound wherever it is most apparent, whether in the chest or nasal passage.

- Continue toning aloud the long OM with each exhale, repeating for 25 to 50 breaths.
- Next, as you exhale, whisper the sound OM. This will be a short, quiet sound rather than the lengthened version of the chanting.
- Repeat this for 25 to 50 breaths.
- Then, shift the short OM sound into your mind. As you exhale, repeat OM in your mind.
- Repeat this for 25 to 50 breaths.
- When you are finished, notice if you feel calmer and more at ease.

Challenge

If you feel uncomfortable or do not have enough privacy to tone a long OM sound, skip this step and just speak the OM aloud quietly rather than chanting a loud, long tone.

Adjustment

If you find that the mantra meditation is resulting in more aggravation, try making less effort. Remember that mantra practice does not need to be perfectly executed to be effective. Dismissing preconceived ideas about what this type of meditation "should" achieve can help with the effectiveness of the technique.

Now that I knew fear, I also knew it was not permanent. As powerful as it was, its grip on me would loosen. It would pass.

— *LOUISE ERDRICH*

Day 12: Worlds of Thought

15–20 minutes

In the same way that digestion is a function of the stomach, thinking is a function of the mind. Thoughts are fueled by both mental habits and the conditions around you. Sometimes thoughts can be very pleasant and entertaining. At other times, you may be tormented by thought. With mindfulness, rather than trying to get rid of your thoughts, you are changing your relationship to your thoughts. You do not have to believe everything that you think! You can start to observe thoughts like sights or sounds: They come and go like everything else in life. In this next meditation, we will take some time to observe thought with curiosity in a non-reactive way.

- Take a moment to make yourself comfortable. Sitting upright will be helpful for this meditation. Turn off your phone and any other electronic devices.
- Remember your intention to investigate thought.
- Take three clearing breaths.

- Start by briefly practicing mindfulness of your breathing. Notice the feeling in your body of breathing in. Observe the feeling in your body of breathing out. Do this for five to seven minutes or until you feel your mind begin to quiet down.
- Begin to notice any thoughts. How can you tell if you are thinking?
- When you notice thinking happening, make a gentle mental note: "Thinking."
- Return to feeling your natural and spontaneous breath between thought waves.
- When you notice thinking again, ask yourself, "What type of thought is happening?" Planning, remembering, judging, problem solving, or analyzing are a few common types of thoughts. Label the thought in your mind.
- Between thought waves, return to feeling the movements of the natural breath.
- When thoughts next arise, again notice the type of thought.
- Return again to the feeling of your breath until the next thought wave arises.

- When thoughts arise again, notice their pace and tone. Are they fast or dreamy? Kind or punishing? Be like a scientist observing thought. Observing thoughts will create a bit of distance from them. You may begin to see that they arise by themselves.
- Return again to the feeling of your breath.
- When thoughts arise again, are you able to tell if the thoughts are in images, words, or a bit of both?
- Return again to the feeling of your breath.
- Thank your mind for all of its efforts to think, care for, and protect you.

Challenge

Sometimes thoughts are so compelling that it becomes difficult to observe them. Instead, you can find yourself swept along rather than observing. Sometimes this can happen if there is an underlying emotion pushing the thoughts along. You can always return to the feeling of your breath in order to calm the mind a bit. And to deal with underlying emotions, you can shift into mindfulness of emotion, the exercise for tomorrow's lesson.

Adjustment

Thoughts arise naturally and often without any premeditation or intentionality. Beware of judging yourself, your thoughts, or the exercise. When this happens, remember that this is just more thinking. Label those thoughts as "judging" in order to give yourself some distance from them. When we get a little distance or space from thoughts, we can see that we don't have to believe every thought.

Day 13: Emotion Motion

15 minutes

Emotions are part of the human condition and therefore part of mindfulness. Mindfulness invites a balanced look at emotions. We are neither trying to get rid of emotions nor trying to indulge them. Often, emotions carry messages or lessons for us that we may not have been aware of. Other times, emotions are simply to be felt so that they can shift and change. Deny emotions, and they color our behavior in unhelpful ways. For example, if I am feeling grumpy and don't notice that I am grumpy, I end up taking the mood out on my partner or anyone else who happens to be around. Conversely, if I am mindfully aware of the grumps, I can communicate that (if needed) or just give myself a little space as necessary. Indulge emotions, and it is like walking into a swamp or quicksand.

In this meditation, you will explore emotion with mindfulness in order to develop an adroit relationship with emotion and grow your emotional intelligence.

Find a quiet place to do this meditation. Reclining or sitting comfortably are both great for this one. Take a moment to remember that you are intending to work with your emotions, not to get rid of or change anything. We start with a body scan. Bring your attention to the top of the head and feel the scalp. Move slowly down your body, opening to sensations from places of ease, tension, and even pain. Relax what is easy to relax. When you get to the bottom of your body, notice the general feel of the entire body. Next, using no particular technique, take a few moments to just be. Then, observe if there are any emotions present. If there are, where do you feel them in your body? Let the awareness be curious like an investigator. Are there images or stories that arise with each emotion?

Does the emotion seem pleasant, unpleasant, or neutral? Does the emotion shift as you bring attention to it? See if you can stay grounded in the physical experience of each emotion in your body. Is there a part of your body that feels neutral or even the opposite emotion? Let the attention be imbued with kindness. You can always place a hand on your chest to support yourself. Notice if anything shifts.

If something becomes overwhelming, open your eyes and look around to help you remember that you are doing a mindfulness exercise. To finish this meditation exploration of emotion, acknowledge with respect the emotions that you have been working with. Then, take three slow, deep breaths.

Challenge

We don't always have an emotion to work with. It is not necessary to create an emotion. You can try to think of a particular situation to bring up an emotion that you would like work with, but you can also save this exercise until you have an emotion you'd like to investigate.

Adjustment

Sometimes emotions can become intense or overwhelming. If this happens, you may need more than solo
mindfulness practice to help you navigate your feelings.
A professional therapist or mental health care professional can help you with emotions and support you in
greater levels of health and thriving.

Day 14: Moments of Gratitude

5 minutes

It is easy for the mind to get stuck in a negative loop,
always complaining and fixating on what is not working.
Gratitude practice helps us shift out of a negative mind-
set. No matter the circumstance, it is always possible to
find something to be grateful for. This is not about being
some sort of inauthentically happy person. Instead, we
can acknowledge difficulties and then make choices to
look toward the gifts of life.

Gratitude practice does not preclude our ability to
make necessary changes. In fact, when we have a more
balanced heart rather than a heart stuck in discourage-
ment or negativity, we have more resilience and capacity

to act with strength and power. Please note that this is not about pretending that injustice does not exist, or ignoring that you may be stuck in a system (familial or societal) that is unhealthy and causes suffering. This is about keeping the mind balanced so that there is greater possibility to move forward with clarity.

- Find a place and time where you will not be interrupted.
- Turn off your phone.
- Remember your intention to be grateful.
- Take three clearing breaths.
- Practice mindful breathing for a few minutes, 50 breaths, or as long as you need to steady the mind and heart and come into the present moment.
- Ask yourself if there is anything that you are grateful for. Look for just one thing. It could be your coffee or your favorite pair of socks! Be open to big and small pockets of gratitude.
- Take a few moments to contemplate the thing or person that you are grateful for.
- Notice what gratitude feels like. Imagine saturating in the feeling of gratitude like a dry

sponge soaking up water or a seedling in the garden drinking in rain.

- If you have time, repeat the exercise for another person or thing.

Challenge

Some days, the mind can be resistant to this exercise. If this happens, be patient with yourself. You might have to get creative to find something that you are grateful for. Do you have a favorite smell? Perhaps you are grateful for the smell of crisp morning air or freshly brewed coffee. Maybe you have a favorite sports team or band that you are grateful for. Try not to judge the thing that you choose! Any place you land is worthy of your gratitude.

Adjustment

If your cup is really empty, this exercise might not feel right. It can be helpful to try a different mindfulness exercise or meditation first, then return to this one. You could try Emotion Motion (see page 88) or Floating in the Present (see page 46).

With mindfulness, you can establish yourself in the present in order to touch the wonders of life that are available in that moment.

— THÍCH NHẤT HẠNH

Mindfulness at Work

This week we will be exploring mindfulness at work. Here, "work" means anything you do to occupy your day—day in and day out. This might be an office job, freelance or gig work, something in the medical profession or service industry, childrearing, or academic pursuits (hey, students!). The point is not *what* you do, but how you relate to your responsibilities.

Recently, I was leading a class on mindfulness when a student spoke up about mindfulness at work. This student was an experienced practitioner who regularly practiced mindfulness in his daily life. He told a story about how the other day at work a crazy deadline arose—six things needed to get done in two hours, and any one of those tasks would take three-plus hours on its own. Returning to his mindfulness practice, he noticed the mounting stress and made the mental note "more, faster" to acknowledge and name these feelings in the moment.

This mindful mental note helped him get a little perspective on the whole thing. He was still facing big deadlines with high expectations, but his mindfulness practice allowed him to see the stress clearly—to observe it rather than be consumed by it. This allowed him to relax into the demands of the situation. Aside from feeling more at ease, he was able to perform better than if he had stayed anxious. This is a beautiful example of the power of mindfulness. With mindfulness, the outer situation may still be charged with intensity, but we can foster an interior experience that allows for more freedom so that we can show up with more skill.

We are now halfway through the 28 days of mindfulness. Good job! We started with mindfulness of the body to anchor you in the primacy of the resource that is the physical body. Next, we moved to mindfulness in the privacy of your home where, in addition to the cultivation of mindfulness of chores, you had time to dive into thoughts, emotions, and gratitude. As we take mindfulness into your work life, we begin to see that the habit of mindfulness can permeate your entire life.

Over the course of the next week, you will practice exercises and meditations that will help you:

- Integrate mindfulness into your work environment in ways that feel non-intrusive and accessible.

- Notice when stress is mounting and take steps to mitigate it.

- Slow down to speed up.

- Improve focus.

Between stimulus and response there is a space.
In that space is our power to choose our response.
In our response lies our growth and our freedom.

— *AUTHOR UNKNOWN*

Day 15: S.T.O.P.

1 minute

What is on your to-do list for today? If your list is anything like mine, it is a list of responsibilities that seems to never end. The word "responsibility" originates from the obsolete French *responsible*, from the Latin *respons*, meaning "answered" or "offered in return," from the verb *respondere*. If anything, mindfulness is a tool to help us respond to the task at hand with skill and fluidity. I have taught this next exercise over and over because so many people find it an effective and easy way to integrate mindful responsiveness into the workday. You can turn to this meditation when the stakes are low or when you feel stress mounting in your body. As you move through the task in front of you—meetings, phone calls, presentations, deadlines, whatever it may be—try using this easy mnemonic to support your responsiveness to that undertaking and your mindfulness: S.T.O.P. This easy mindfulness reminder is an acronym for:

- S - Stop what you are doing.
- T - Take a mindful breath (or several). Breathe in, knowing you are breathing in; breathe out, knowing you are breathing out.

- O - Observe the present moment by noting how your body is feeling, your thoughts, where you are, and what you are doing.
- P - Proceed with attention to the task at hand.

Challenge

As with any mindfulness exercise, the biggest challenge is remembering to do it. To help you remember to S.T.O.P., you can set a timer or find a mindfulness S.T.O.P. buddy. Every time you remember to S.T.O.P., you'll feel the positive benefits and also be more likely to remember to practice it again.

Adjustment

You can adjust the number of mindful breaths that you take on step T, depending on how much time and emotional space you need from whatever you are taking a break from.

Day 16: Write, Pause, Send

5–10 seconds

A few years ago, I was on a monthlong mindfulness retreat in Myanmar. Usually on retreats such as this one, accessing the Internet is not allowed, whether by phone or other electronic device. But every day on this retreat there was a period of "Internet mindfulness." We all gathered in a room, and I used the old-fashioned dial-up connection to send emails to loved ones back home. I would pause with attention every time before hitting the send button. This habit carried over into my life long after I came home. (I must say that it has saved me more than once from sending something that I would later regret.) Taking a breath and noticing where you are—what is happening in and around you—before pressing send can turn emailing into a mindfulness practice.

> Every time you are about to hit send on an email, pause. Take a breath. Notice that you are about to send an email! Take another deep breath. Observe the feeling of your body, noticing any tension or places of ease. Make sure the email is in alignment with your purpose. Then do it! You are ready to mindfully press send.

Challenge

This one takes time and dedication to do consistently, but it eventually becomes habitual. Keep working on developing the habit in a steady way. You can try ending your emails with a new sign-off to remind you to do it.

Adjustment

Try this with text messages, instant messages on platforms such as Gmail or Slack, or even social media posts.

Day 17: Stress Buster

1–4 minutes

We spend so much time at work, with all of the accompanying pressure to perform and accomplish. (This applies to all occupational hats.) Sometimes stress gets the best of all of us. This next meditation cuts through tension, allowing for better attention to detail and better results. It may seem counterintuitive when the pressure is high, but taking a several minute break gives us the freedom to reset, helping us show up and do what needs to be done.

- Stop what you are doing and physically (if you can; if not, mentally) turn away from the activity.
- Close your eyes. If you have glasses, take them off. You can also cover your eyes with your hands.
- Inhale slowly to a count of four.
- Exhale to a count of eight.
- Repeat this for one to four minutes.
- Say something kind to yourself, such as "Good job, [name]," or "May I be peaceful."

Challenge

Sometimes it can be challenging to exhale for eight counts. Let the breath fine-tune itself to be just the right length—whatever suits your needs. You can lengthen or shorten it; just keep the exhale twice as long as the inhale.

Adjustment

Depending on your work environment and responsibilities, it may not be workable for you to close your eyes for a minute. Instead, you can do this exercise without closing your eyes. For example, you can do this exercise in "stealth" mode with your eyes open during a meeting.

Day 18: Beginnings and Endings

1–2 minutes

On a meditation retreat, a teacher instructed me to notice every time something was finished, whether it was a thought, a breath, walking out of a room, or even (once home) a conversation. It was a truly transformative practice, as it allowed me to see when something was ending and, therefore, when another moment was beginning. This practice sharpened my mindfulness, enabling me to better settle into the flow of experience. By letting go of the past moment, I was able to be fully present. Noticing beginnings and endings creates healthy boundaries with work and allows you to move more fully into the present by entirely letting go of what has passed.

Every time you start a task, such as caring for a child, starting a meeting, ringing up a customer, or opening a book, notice that you are beginning an activity. Make a mental note that you are putting aside whatever has come before and are now working on the task in front of you. If you enjoy setting intentions, set an intention for the new activity. When you are finished with the task, make a mental note that you are finished, acknowledging its end. Give yourself permission to put down the work associated with the completed task. This includes putting down the mental preoccupation with the task that is now finished.

Challenge

Mentally putting down work when we are finished can be challenging. If you need help with this, try creating a small ritual like making a mental note ("I am done now"), or even taking a drink of water to clear yourself.

Sometimes putting work down is hard because there is an emotional charge. You can address this with some other mindfulness exercises and meditations, such as the Body Scan (see page 40), Emotion Motion (see page 88), or Mantra Medicine (see page 81).

Adjustment

Your work life may be blurry, starting and stopping many times a but, you can still do this exercise. At the end of the day, put aside the work you've done, and give your full attention to whatever you do next.

Few of us ever live in the present, we are forever anticipating what is to come or remembering what has gone.

— *LOUIS L'AMOUR*

Day 19: Body Connectivity

2 minutes

When life gets going and one is deeply immersed in work, often the connection to the body is lost along with all that it can do to support you. We have so many habits that get us through our workdays, but without the body, we would not be at work. The body is never anywhere but in the present moment. The body's life force and wisdom are both available through mindfulness of the body. Try this exercise to help ground and center your-self throughout your busiest days.

- Take one to three deep breaths.
- Remember your intention to practice mindfulness for your well-being.
- Notice whatever it is that your body is doing, whether sitting or standing.
- Check in and see if you are hungry, tired, or need to use the restroom. Maybe you just need to close your eyes for a moment. Take care of your physical needs if you can. If you are in a situation where you need to hold off on something, mentally tell your body that you will tend to it as soon as you can.

- Note if there are areas of your body that feel comfortable or strong.
- Thank your body for supporting you, saying to yourself, "May I be balanced."

Challenge

It can be hard to tell if your body is hungry or even if it needs to use the restroom, especially if you tend to ignore its signals. With practice, this will become easier. Take some time to listen to the wisdom of your body and what it has to offer you.

Adjustment

If tension has accumulated in your body, even just a little movement or stretching can get things loose again. If you are able to, stand up and notice your feet and legs under you. Try moving your shoulders, neck, and head, welcoming the sensations of movement. Lift your arms up or swing them around as you feel into your shoulders. Small movements are fine, but if you can make the movements a little bigger, that will help with releasing tension.

Day 20: The Task at Hand

1 minute–1 hour

Multitasking can feel important and unavoidable. You may have habits of doing more than one thing at a time, and you may even be encouraged or required to multi-task as part of your job. However, research indicates that we are not as successful as we may think when we try to do multiple activities at once. In fact, productivity can go down as much as 40 percent when we get stuck in a world of multitasking. Doing one thing at a time allows us to be more focused and productive. Follow these steps to begin focusing on the task at hand.

- Take several clearing breaths.
- Note your intention to do one thing at a time.
- Set a block of time to work on a task.
- Turn off any alarms and notifications that you can for the amount of time that you have set aside.
- Notice what factors lead to distraction. Are you stuck on how to proceed? Bored? Note these factors without judgment.
- If you move away from the task, try to catch yourself and gently direct yourself back with as little self-recrimination as possible.

- When the time that you have set aside is finished, take one breath before moving to the next task.

Challenge

Distractions can be built into your work or life situation. Give yourself permission to stay loose around this exercise. Don't expect to be perfectly focused or for the world to provide the perfect conditions. We are never able to control everything (and everyone) at all times, and circumstances might limit your ability to focus on a single task at a time. If you face such circumstances, try adjusting the amount of time you stay on one task to smaller increments. For example, if you are waiting tables, focus on just filling water cups or taking an order. Creativity always applies.

Adjustment

Mindfulness is not meant to exclude others or the daily demands of your life from your attention. If you find that you need to pay attention to someone else during this exercise, like your child, just shift the mindfulness to whatever arises.

Day 21: Clarity in Speech

At least 6 seconds

When I started working with mindful speech, one of my teachers, Anna Douglas, instructed me to check in with my reason for speaking in the moment right before I spoke. I learned from this practice that when my reasons for speaking were manipulative or antagonistic, the words would come out sideways and cause problems. I had to be brave and honest to admit to myself that sometimes my heat-of-the-moment intention wasn't kind. Once I brought greater awareness to this practice, I was able to speak with more clarity and power.

Communication can be a source of great frustration when it goes wrong and can lead to all sorts of difficulty with work. This exercise will support your capacity to speak with clarity while hard at work—and in other areas of your daily life.

Before you speak, take a moment to pause. What is your purpose for speaking? Do you need to set a boundary or communicate a delicate issue? Check in with your reasons for sharing. Do you have any underlying feelings, negative or positive, about this communication? It is not a problem if you do; just notice with mindfulness if that is the case and if your intentions are mixed. Sometimes we have a general intention of kindness, but in the moment feelings such as irritation or anger override the original kind intention. If you are too heated up, consider pausing further before you speak. This pause could be for just one breath, or it could be for longer, such as a few days or even weeks. When you are ready, as best you can, speak in a way that supports your highest intentions.

Challenge

It can be hard to know what your purpose for speaking is in any one moment. Start slowly with this one, practicing in less charged situations. If you find that you are unable or unwilling to notice your purpose for speaking, that may be a clue that more meditation may be necessary. You are under no obligation to do this exercise to be "nice" or to stifle your voice. The goal is to help you speak with more clarity, resulting in better communication.

Adjustment

Sometimes you may need to say something to someone who has power over you, such as your boss. It can be difficult to figure out what to say and how to say it. Spend some time reflecting on what you want to say. Practice writing it down, fine tuning the words to be both truthful and respectful. Make sure that what you want to say is useful to yourself or others in the situation. Then, find the right time to say what needs to be said. In this way, you will speak whatever it is that needs to be said in a timely manner with respect and clarity. Your speech will have integrity and power.

*Kind words can be short and easy to speak,
but their echoes are truly endless.*

— *MOTHER TERESA*

Mindfulness in the World

In this final week of the four-week mindfulness plan, you are now prepared to explore mindfulness beyond the boundaries of work and home, taking your mind, body, spirit—your wholeness—with you as you go. Here, you will build on what you have already learned from your practice, incorporating the same themes of kindness, awareness, and curiosity.

You may have already started to notice that part of the magic of this practice arises from small mindful moments adding up as you weave them throughout your day. It is like filling up a bucket one droplet at a time. At any one moment, a single drop of mindfulness may not seem that big or important, but eventually your bucket will be full—maybe even overflowing.

The practice of mindfulness will permeate your life, allowing you to remember the wisdom of the bigger picture and shift your relationship to your experience and your life. Mindfulness of your body continues to be a through line of awareness as you explore your life behind the wheel of a car, on public transportation, or at the park. This chapter also offers exercises to bring deliberate kindness and respect into your relationships with yourself and those around you. By the end of this week, you will be able to:

- Explore mindfulness in any environment

- Practice mindfulness with the heart qualities of respect and care

- Bring your practice into your relationship with others

Meditation is the journey from sound to silence, from movement to stillness, from a limited identity to unlimited space.

— *SRI SRI RAVI SHANKAR*

Day 22: Simply Sound

10 minutes

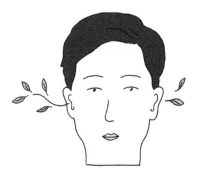

I just moved from an urban area to the countryside in Northern California, and the soundscape is so different here. When meditating with sound, I used to be surrounded by people, the neighbor's music, cars going by, sirens, and planes overhead. In a rural environment, meditating with sound includes birds, wind in the trees, and an occasional dog barking. Because we are surrounded by sound all of the time and sound comes and goes on its own, it can be a great primary object for meditation. For this meditation, instead of the breath, sound will be the place where we draw our attention. If available, try to choose a place where there is silence and ambient sound, rather than a loud radio, TV, or music.

- Find a comfortable posture that is upright and at ease.
- Note your intention to practice mindfulness of sound.
- Take three deep breaths.
- Start by scanning your body for any areas of tension and relaxing the tension that easily relaxes. Please note that not all tension can relax on command. Do what you can.
- Relax your body one part at a time, cycling through your entire body two or three times.
- Shift your attention to sound. Rather than listening to the content of sound, simply notice that you are listening.
- Observe that sound is happening.
- Notice the arising and passing of sound.
- Notice the space between sounds.
- When your mind wanders, note your wandering mind.
- Gently bring yourself back to listening to the sounds.

Challenge

Sounds can distract you, leading to tangential thinking or even pulling the attention too far into the content of the sound. Try doing this meditation outdoors in a park, next to an open window, or somewhere where ambient noise is prominent but not too loud or soft. Try to avoid music with lyrics (or music in general) so that you can stay focused on sound rather than the content of the sound.

Adjustment

If you are deaf or hard of hearing, try this meditation with a different sense, such as touch on the skin. For example, observe the contact of clothes and air on the skin. Keep bringing the attention to the feeling of contact or touch rather than thoughts about the sensations.

Day 23: Self-Compassion Break

5 minutes

Today we will work with self-compassion, which nurtures resilience and builds the capacity to meet the challenges of everyday life. Sometimes the idea of self-compassion can be confusing and unclear. Self-compassion does not mean over-indulgence or neglecting loved ones. We are self-compassionate when we act as our own best friend by offering kindness, respect, and support to ourselves. Kristin Neff, a researcher at the University of Texas, has studied and written extensively about self-compassion. This exercise is one that she developed.

- Bring to mind a difficult situation in your life. This can be an emotional, physical, work, or relationship-related situation. Take a little time to see if you can feel the discomfort in your body and/or mind.
- Use your mindfulness to note that this is a challenge or difficulty. Mindfulness sees with clarity what is actually happening. You can make a mental note, such as "This hurts," "Suffering is like this," or "This is stressful."
- Remember that difficulty and pain are part of life. Say to yourself, "I am not alone," "Others feel similarly," or "Everyone struggles."
- Take at least one action. Place a hand on your heart or make a mental note, such as "May I be held in compassion." You can also ask yourself what might be helpful for you to hear or do to support yourself in this challenge or difficulty.

Challenge

Especially during times of high activity or stress, it can be hard to know when something difficult is arising in our minds and bodies. We may not even notice that we need a self-compassion break. Try this exercise if you are feeling grumpy, overwhelmed, stressed, or even angry. You can also practice this skill with very small difficulties, such as burning dinner or forgetting to respond to a text.

Adjustment

You might feel that the situation you've brought to mind is so large and immediate that this practice seems like a waste of time—that your difficulty is too overwhelming to acknowledge. Remember that when we are centered and present, when we cultivate awareness, the skills needed to navigate challenges will be more readily available.

What Is Self-Compassion?

Self-compassion is the care and action that you show yourself in the face of challenge, struggle, and pain. It is as ordinary as turning the pillow over to a cool spot for yourself in the deep of the night. At other times, self-compassion requires us to speak up for ourselves or to change an outer circumstance. Most often, it is as simple as a shift in attitude from denial or self-criticism to support and concern.

Kristin Neff, a researcher and author at the University of Texas, discovered the teachings of compassion through her mindfulness practice and decided to do extensive research on the topic of self-compassion. Her research clearly shows that people who are more self-compassionate tend to be measurably less anxious and depressed. Self-compassion leads to better emotional resilience and capacity to bounce back from mistakes.

When we are self-compassionate, we act in our own best interests to support our emotional and physical health, especially in the face of pain or difficulty. The practices of mindfulness that you are engaging with here are in themselves acts of self-compassion. Mindfulness will help you notice when you have lost the thread of self-compassion. This takes practice but is well worth the effort. Try the following ritual to let go of patterns of self-criticism:

- Notice when your mind is filled with negative self-talk. If you are alone, you can try speaking your inner monologue out loud. Notice with mindfulness—without judgment—that this is happening.
- Observe how you feel physically and emotionally.
- Take one very deep breath in through the nose and exhale slowly out of the mouth.
- Touch yourself on the chest, face, or hand in a gesture of support.
- Say to yourself, "May I be safe from inner harm."

Day 24: Yield to the Present

10 minutes

The average American commutes more than 200 hours a year. And that doesn't count travel for errands and recreational activities. With so much time in transit, it makes sense to practice mindfulness when we're on the go—on a plane, on a train, on a bus, or in the car.

Elaine, a student and resident of the traffic-clogged Bay Area, reported to me that practicing mindfulness of driving helped her shift her perspective on driving from a competitive stance to an understanding that we are all part of traffic; traffic is not just everyone else. For me, mindful driving helps me release stress when I am stuck for long periods of time in the car.

> When you get into the car, take a breath and confirm your intention to practice mindfulness. The first few times you try this exercise, turn off any music or the radio. Check in with your body before you buckle up by feeling your back against the car seat. Remember to keep your attention focused on what you are doing. As you begin to drive, notice that you are driving. Observe what's happening around you, whether it is the flow of traffic, sounds in your environment,

or how you check the mirrors or regulate your speed. Be aware that you are aware of your environment. Track any emotional responses, such as pleasure, irritation, or frustration. Continue to feel your back end on the seat and your hands on the wheel. Note the feeling of the car as an extension of you. When you are finished, thank the car for working and thank the infrastructure of the road system.

Challenge

If you find yourself rushing, notice why. Are you late? Do you have to rush even if you are late? Perhaps you can go at a steady rate and still get to wherever you are going. Consider that driving is a cooperative event, not a competition.

Adjustment

Maybe you don't drive but bike or walk instead. To do this exercise while walking or biking, start in the same way by confirming your intention to practice mindfulness, then checking in with your body. Keep your attention focused on what you are doing as you step forward or hop on the bike. Observe yourself tracking the environment. Continue to notice that you are seeing the traffic and your surroundings. Notice the feeling in the feet and legs as they power you forward. Track any emotional responses, such as pleasure, annoyance, or frustration. Keep bringing your attention back to the feeling of your body as it walks or rides. When you are finished, thank your body for functioning so well—it is a gift to have a body that can walk or bike.

Before starting the car,

I know where I am going.

The car and I are one.

If the car goes fast, I go fast.

— *THÍCH NHẤT HẠNH*

Day 25: All Aboard!

2 minutes

All over the world, trains hum and thrum, taking people here and there. When you step onto a train, you join the millions of people worldwide also traveling from A to B. And whether you are on your regular commute or going on an errand, the betwixt-and-between train environment provides the perfect backdrop for a moment of mindfulness. On the train, there is not much else going on, since it's between coming and going. Rather than playing a game on your phone or checking social media, tune up your mindfulness. For today's meditation, we will be mindful of the activity of each sense rather than what in particular is sensed. For example, rather than paying attention to what you are seeing, you can pay attention to the fact that seeing is happening.

> Find a place to sit or stand as far from the doors as possible. Make sure that your phone is safely tucked away for the duration of the meditation. In this meditation, you will move through your senses one at a time, observing the particular sense that is in action. Begin with sound. There will be layers of sound around you. Some sounds will be close; some will be

further away. As you listen, notice that you are hearing. Next, move to sight. Notice that you are seeing. You might be able to see inside and outside the train. Avoid getting too caught up in the details of what you are seeing. Stay more with the fact that seeing is happening. Now, notice the touch and temperature of the air and clothes on your skin. Be aware of what your hands and feet are touching. Touch is happening. Move to taste—is there a residual taste on your tongue? Do you have gum or candy in your mouth? Can you still taste your toothpaste or maybe your morning coffee? Notice if tasting is happening. Finally, what are the smells around you? Again, without getting too caught up in the actual smells, observe that smelling is happening.

You can cycle through your senses again as many times as you like. Try to avoid judging or getting too caught up in any of the things you hear, see, touch, taste, or smell. You are here simply to observe the senses in action. If someone unexpectedly jostles you, just note that touch happened. When an announcement comes on, note that hearing is happening. Be flexible to what is going on around you.

Challenge

You may find yourself reacting to the sights and smells around you on the train. This is not a problem if you are aware of it when it happens. Just note with kindness, "Judging mind is like this." It is only a problem when we judge ourselves for reacting or completely getting lost in reactivity. Once you have noticed reactivity, continue on to the next sense.

Adjustment

Try this in an airport, on an airplane, on a bus, or in the waiting room of the doctor's office.

Day 26: Stealth Benevolence

5–7 minutes

On the first day of a new meditation class, I always ask my students to consider the possibility that all the other people in the room are friendly. Usually everyone laughs with recognition at how easy it is to adopt a defensive or negative assumption that others are greedy, unjust, or unkind.

This next exercise challenges that assumption, asking us to retrain our attitude of kindness and benevolence toward others. This exercise is not about being nice, getting people to like you, or letting go of appropriate boundaries. It is simply an exercise designed to train the mind toward kindness to all, including ourselves.

> Today you get to pretend that you are a benevolent spirit offering blessings to all that you see! You can do this for anyone or everyone that you see in your environment. You can also send love to a family member, a friend, or even someone with whom you've lost touch. Decide what kind wishes you would like to bestow today. Maybe you will wish health, peace, or safety to all of the people that you see. It can be helpful to remember that every person was once a baby or child. At the end of the day, notice if you feel more connected to and empathic for others. (It's okay if you don't; just take note of where you are.)

Challenge

The mind generally is full of thoughts, stories, and judgments of people that we see around us. It is wonderful to notice when this happens, because then we can see more clearly that our internal biases and snap judgments may not be true. You do not have to stop these thoughts, stories, and judgments from arising. All that you have to do is acknowledge their presence so that you do not react. Consider the possibility that your thoughts, stories, and judgments are not true.

Adjustment

You might encounter resistance to this exercise. It can even bring up angry or sad feelings if we think about people or situations that have caused us pain in the past. If that happens, it does not mean that you are doing the exercise wrong. Your cup simply might be empty that day. If this is the case, offer benevolent blessings to yourself instead of others throughout your day. Fine tune the blessing or wish to resonate with you. You can shift to others once you are feeling more resilient.

Day 27: Undivided Attention

5 minutes

We pay attention to what we are interested in. Some might say that we pay attention to people and things that we love. Yet, with the evolution of the smartphone, our attention has shifted away from our environment and our loved ones to the world of the screen. Technology has brought new avenues of connectivity and progress, but at the same time, it has distracted us from the people right in front of us.

For this meditation, put down your device and any other distractions, giving your full attention to the person in front of you. When you do this, you are signaling your respect and care. This can improve relationships and the overall quality of your life.

- Set an intention to give your full attention to a friend, family member, or loved one for a specific amount of time.
- Notice your body language. Turn your body toward the person you are paying attention to.
- Say "no" to distractions and interruptions, even from your own mind. Keep bringing your attention back to the present moment.

- Listen first. When you listen, give your full attention rather than planning what you want to say or do.
- Pause before rushing to speak.
- Respond with curiosity; keep the focus on your loved one.

Challenge

Especially the first time you practice this meditation, keep it simple. If you make a big production about doing this exercise, it will turn into something more about you than your loved one.

Adjustment

Adjust what you do to meet the needs of each friend or loved one. For example, with a child, you can let them lead with play. With someone who is ill, you might need to do more of the talking.

*Anything will give up its secrets
if you love it enough.*

— *GEORGE WASHINGTON CARVER*

Day 28: Ordinary Treasures

1–2 minutes

So often we rush through life without actually being present to all of the beauty that surrounds us. I am not necessarily talking about picture-perfect-postcard beauty but instead the more ordinary kind, such as the sparkle in a child's eye or the blue sky filled with big, puffy white clouds. Taking time to notice someone playing music on the street or the striking color of paint on the wall can seat us more directly in the present and keep us from losing ourselves in waves of thought and anxiety. Today's meditation will help you look around and see what the world has to offer you.

- Set an intention to notice as many beautiful or pleasing things in your environment as you can all day long.
- As the day goes on, let your eye be drawn to anything that strikes you as pleasing or even beautiful. This can be anything—a color, a picture, a tree.
- Also notice anything pleasing or beautiful in sound, taste, or touch.

- As you do this, be aware that you are aware.
- If there is pleasure in this exercise, be aware of this too.

Challenge

If the mind is wrapped up in something, this exercise can be hard to do. Start really small. Take a break and begin with a mantra or mindful breathing to center yourself. Then, look around and see if anything strikes you.

Adjustment

Do this exercise somewhere in nature, perhaps a park. Let your eye take in the shades of green. Look up into the sky. Observe animals.

Rejoicing in ordinary things is not sentimental or trite. It actually takes guts.

— *PEMA CHÖDRÖN*

Bonus: Loving-Kindness Meditation

10 minutes

Loving-kindness Meditation is a type of meditation designed to support the practitioner in the development of a kind and friendly attitude toward themselves and the people around them. With practice, a willingness to not harm—even in the mind—can be developed. The word loving-kindness might evoke in you visions of sappy, soft romanticism. But loving-kindness is better understood as friendliness, unconditional benevolence, or even respect. In English when we say that we "love" something, often we mean that we like it a lot. For example, I love chocolate and striped socks. However, the quality of loving-kindness is not about liking. Loving-kindness instead is about respecting and refraining from harm. This is a fierce and strong remedy for the habits of irritation, spitefulness, and hostility. Over time, we begin to learn to let ourselves off of the hook so that we can create a friendly inner environment that can then ripple out into the community.

In the following meditation, you will bring together the full power of your mind through intention and the strength of unconditional benevolence. In general, loving-kindness meditation starts with the self, then moves out to the people around you (even difficult people), and then expands to the broader world. This meditation focuses on loving-kindness toward a loved one and the self. You can use this meditation regularly if you would like to work with patterns of self-criticism and low self-confidence. You can also do this for a few minutes at the end of your daily practice.

- Make yourself as comfortable as possible.
- Remember your intention of respect and care for yourself.

- Place a hand palm down on the center of your chest, then stack your other hand on top of it in a gesture of warmth and support.
- Take a slow breath, feeling your hands and your chest. You can keep your hands where they are or let them rest wherever they feel comfortable.
- Bring to mind someone that you feel friendly toward. This could be a pet, a child in your life, or a teacher—someone who you have an uncomplicated relationship with and who it is easy for you to feel warmth or gratitude toward.
- Imagine this person or being smiling. If it is a dog, maybe its tail is wagging; if it is a cat, maybe it is purring. Say this person's (or being's) name in your mind.
- In your mind say to this being, "May you be safe and protected." This means safety from harmful inner mental states and outer danger in the world. Next, in your mind say to this being, "May you be free from pain." This means freedom from both mental and physical pain. "May you be happy."

- Tune into the meaning of the phrases as you say them.
- Repeat these phrases 2 to 10 times. Keep the person or being you are sending the phrases toward in mind, whether by calling an image or sense of them to mind or holding their name in your mind. Continue connecting to the meaning of the phrases.
- Imagine that this person is now sending you blessings. You might have a sense of them smiling at you or touching you.
- Say to yourself, "May I be safe and protected," while allowing yourself to connect to the meaning of the words. Next, in your mind repeat the words, "May I be free from pain." And finally, "May I be happy."
- Repeat these phrases in your mind slowly 2 to 10 times. If it helps, you can imagine yourself as a small child or baby.
- Consider that, just like you, all beings everywhere want to be happy.
- Say to yourself, "May all beings be safe and protected. May all beings be free from pain. May all beings be happy."

Challenge

Anything can and will happen during this style of meditation. You might feel nothing, you might feel numb, or you might feel anger. You might go on long, discursive trains of thought or stories. When any of this happens, use your mindfulness. Make a gentle note of what is happening. Instead of judging yourself or your experience, simply notice with the curiosity of a scientist. You might say to yourself, "Oh! Look, thinking is like this." And then out of compassion for yourself, bring your attention right back to the phrases.

Adjustment

You can fine tune the phrases to be more in alignment with what has meaning for you. The idea is to be general rather than specific, as this is about the cultivation of inner goodwill rather than a prayer for a particular outcome like a pay raise. Some alternate phrases are:

"May I accept myself just as I am."

"May I be kind to myself."

"May I be at peace."

Ongoing
Practice

Congratulations! You have worked your way through four weeks of mindfulness meditations and practices. You've focused on the body and practiced home, at work, and out in the world. The next step is up to you. Like all things that are worth doing, mindfulness takes repeated effort and commitment.

With this plan, as in life, growth flows in spirals rather than on a linear path. The practice of mindfulness ebbs and flows in the same way. You might feel the power of the continuity of practice after this month's journey and be inspired to continue. Or you might have stopped after reading the first paragraph of this book. It is normal to weave in and out of mindfulness practice. Know that you can always start again right where you are.

Perhaps the biggest tragedy in our lives is that freedom is possible, yet we can pass our years trapped in the same old patterns . . . We may want to love other people without holding back, to feel authentic, to breathe in the beauty around us, to dance and sing. Yet each day we listen to inner voices that keep our life small.

— *TARA BRACH*

Setting Expectations

There will be periods of time when you will be especially focused on your practice. You may find yourself practicing regularly and discovering great support for yourself in life. These periods of deep practice will continue to support you when your practice wavers. It turns out that once you have practiced regularly for some time, you carry your practice with you even on those days—or weeks—that you forget to practice. The power of mindfulness is cumulative. Regular practice over time is like charging up your battery, and when you come to times without daily practice, you can draw on that charge. Over time, you will begin to notice when your "battery" is low, whether through mood or lack of resiliency. You will know that it is time to get back to mindfulness to recharge.

At other times, even when you know the advantages of practicing, it can be so hard to actually practice. When this happens, give yourself permission to start again, on any day at any time. The only place and time to make change is here in this moment. We cannot change the past; we can only be alive in the moment. The way to a better future is by acting in this moment. Once we take care of the present moment, the future takes care of itself.

Bringing Yourself Back

When you lose the thread of practice, start again with as little recrimination or storytelling as possible. Mindfulness invites us into the present moment, which is always available to us. Your mind will wander—your life may even wander—but as soon as you have noticed the wandering, you are again practicing mindfulness. That's it. Just notice what is happening with curiosity, non-reactivity, and kindness. At that point, you might be inspired to take a mindful breath. Taking one breath with mindfulness will make it more likely that you will remember to take another.

Every day, the mind is full of stories and thoughts. These stories and thoughts can impact your quality of life, your resilience, and your ability to be effective in life. However, you don't need to stop your thoughts to deal with these difficulties. With mindfulness, we have more capacity to make choices rather than living in reactivity to our thoughts and stories. These choices include many of the practices that you have already explored with this book, such as taking a mindful breath, turning your attention to something in your environment, or taking a self-compassion break. Bringing yourself back one moment at a time is the practice of mindfulness.

One Breath at a Time

One of the beauties of mindfulness is that the principles are the same whether we are in a period of ease or we are facing extensive challenges. Of course, it is easier to practice when things are less stressful, but you might not have that choice. The key is to start small and start simple. One moment, one breath. All that mindfulness requires is to meet each moment with as much attention as is possible for you in that moment. Remember to feel your breath. Notice the feeling of your feet and legs. Turn your attention to what you see around you. Notice that you are alive.

When things heat up and the present moment is painful, call on the quality of kindness. It can be so difficult to stay in any one moment if it is a painful one. Remember that it is human to feel pain and experience difficulty. You can place a hand on your chest or say a compassionate phrase to yourself, such as, "May I be held in compassion." In fact, one of the skills we develop through meditation is the ability to stay steady when faced with the monkey mind, pain, or emotional challenges. Meditation is a place to learn to hold yourself in kindness even when in pain.

Before you know kindness as the deepest thing inside, you must know sorrow as the other deepest thing.

— *NAOMI SHIHAB NYE*

The Next 30 Days

Anything can happen in the next 30 days. As you move through these next weeks of your life, things will go up and down. You change, I change, the world changes. However, one thing is for certain: Mindfulness can support you as you sail through life. The kindness, curiosity, non-reactivity, non-striving, and self-reliance of mindfulness that you have been practicing over the past month will continue to sustain you, especially as you find ways to continue practicing.

When you are developing your ongoing meditation practice, remember that five minutes a day is better than *no* minutes a day. Avoid setting yourself up for failure by expecting yourself to practice meditation for an unrealistic amount of time. As you begin to see the benefits of meditation, you will be more inclined to meditate. At that point you can slowly begin to increase the amount of time you spend in your practice.

It's also helpful to remember that resistance is part of meditation practice. Although you should never be in physical pain or push yourself to emotional distress from the practice of mindfulness (please stop and breathe if either of these happen!), the practice does not have to feel "pleasant" or "joyful" to be beneficial.

There are no shortcuts to any place worth going.

— *BEVERLY SILLS*

The Role of Resistance

Struggle and resistance are part of being human. When things are heating up, choose any exercise or meditation that appeals to you rather than going for the toughest or longest one. The goal is simply to arrive where you are. It is very important to add compassion and kindness to your practices, especially when things feel difficult or challenging. Allow yourself to be understanding and open to forgiveness, even and especially for yourself. Resistance is not an experience to judge; it is simply part of life.

Sometimes we may have the view that mindfulness should be easy—especially after practice. Other times we may feel like mindfulness is always difficult. Either of these views may be true some of the time, but neither is true all of the time. Mindfulness will flow and feel like a natural fit at some times, and at other times it may seem like the hardest practice in the world. Don't let your mind get stuck in either view. Mindfulness is never any one thing, and neither are you. Your life is changing, and you are changing, too. Your experience of the practice of mindfulness will shift. Don't give up if it seems hard—just start again in the exact place that you are.

The science shows that we most effectively make changes in our lives when we focus on creating the conditions necessary for change rather than relying on willpower to push us through. Joining a mindfulness meditation group can be helpful to this end. Most people report that having a weekly group to practice with supports them throughout the whole week. Enlist a willing friend to be a gratitude buddy or mindfulness pal. Use an app like Insight Timer or Headspace. You might also consider attending a silent meditation retreat to deepen your understanding and kick-start your daily practice. I have included some resources at the end of this book (see page 167) to get you started.

Expanding Your Daily Practice

The exercises and meditations in this book are a launching pad for you to incorporate mindfulness into your life. Please feel free to expand your practice as you see fit. The most important next step is to trust yourself and trust the practice. Be curious and creative. Here are just a few ways to find mindfulness in the everyday:

- Peel an orange with mindfulness. Notice the smell, the texture, and the color of the fruit. Notice if you salivate. Be aware that you are peeling an orange while you are peeling it.

- Eat a piece of chocolate or something that you find rather delicious. Place the food in your mouth and taste the flavor. Notice how your tongue and mouth move. Attend to the texture and allow the food to melt.

- Visit 30 seconds of mindful breathing. Breathe in, knowing that you are breathing in, and breathe out, knowing that you are breathing out.

- Each time you answer the phone, take a breath and remember that you are answering the phone. Then give the caller your full attention.

- Practice mindfulness in bed before going to sleep. Put your phone down and turn off the TV. Take a few minutes to relax your body, starting at the feet and moving up to the head. Then, breathe deeply for a few minutes.

- Upon waking, while still in bed, notice that you have woken up. Do a deliberate stretch like a cat. Notice the room around you and your body in the bed.

- Touch and stroke your own hand. Use one hand to touch the other. Feel both sides of the touch by feeling both hands. Let this comfort you.

- Observe one thing in your environment. Look around you. What do you see?

- Look at a flower or plant with attention. Let nature sustain you with its beauty. Rather than just glancing, really take it in.

- Notice three ordinary objects in your environment that you are grateful for. You might be grateful for the fire alarm. I appreciate the comfy desk chair given to me by a friend that I am sitting on right now.

Harmony, Grace, and Gratitude

We all practice mindfulness out of care for our lives, health, and well-being. Your aspiration to practice mindfulness is an expression of love and care for yourself. Call to mind your own inspiration for reading this book and taking up the challenge of mindfulness. Through your practice, you may have started to see for yourself that peace comes not from outer circumstance but through our own heart and mind. It is my deepest hope that you have enjoyed for yourself the firsthand benefits of a mindfulness practice.

May you know peace and joy.

It turns out that we also practice for others, because what we do and how we are matters in this world. May all the benefits of our collective practice of mindfulness spread far and wide. Thank you for your practice of mindfulness and your efforts to care for yourself and the world that you live in.

May all beings everywhere know peace and joy.

Resources

Books

Buddha's Brain: The Practical Neuroscience of Happiness, Love, and Wisdom, Rick Hanson with Richard Mendius

Radical Acceptance: Embracing Your Life with the Heart of a Buddha, Tara Brach

Self-Compassion: The Proven Power of Being Kind to Yourself, Kristin Neff

When Things Fall Apart: Heart Advice for Difficult Times, Pema Chödrön

Silent Retreats

Insight Meditation Society, Barre, MA, Dharma.org

Spirit Rock Meditation Center, Woodacre, CA, SpiritRock.org

Vallecitos Mountain Retreat Center, Tusas Mountains, NM, Vallecitos.org

Sitting Groups

Look for a local group. Search online for "mindfulness meditation" or "Vipassana meditation."

Audio Recordings of Talks and Guided Meditations

Audio Dharma, AudioDharma.org

Dharma Seed, DharmaSeed.org

Websites

Dr. Kristin Neff: Self-Compassion, Self-Compassion.org

Dr. Rick Hanson: The Neuroscience of Lasting Happiness, RickHanson.net

Jack Kornfield: Author, Buddhist Practitioner, JackKornfield.com

Tara Brach, PhD: Psychologist, Author, and Teacher of Meditation, TaraBrach.com

UCLA Mindful Awareness Research Center, UCLAHealth.org/marc

Apps

10% Happier
Headspace
Insight Timer

References

Kabat-Zinn, Jon. *Wherever You Go, There You Are: Mindfulness Meditation in Everyday Life*. New York: Hachette Books, 1994.

Neff, Kristin. *Self-Compassion: The Proven Power of Being Kind to Yourself*. New York: William Morrow, 2011.

About the Author

Ashley Sharp lives in Fort Bragg, California, among the redwood trees with her husband, artist Joe Murphy. An ardent lifetime learner, Sharp has attended years of meditation and mindfulness courses, retreats, and workshops everywhere—from India and Myanmar to California and Massachusetts. She has been teaching yoga, meditation, and mindfulness for 20 years and founded Insight Richmond, a community-based meditation group. She teaches retreats at Refuge at Pudding Creek, her home in Fort Bragg. More information about Ashley and her teachings can be found at AshleySharp.net.

CPSIA information can be obtained
at www.ICGtesting.com
Printed in the USA
JSHW022000130820
7270JS00005B/8